# Social Work Licensing Clinical Exam Practice Test

**Dawn Apgar, PhD, LSW, ACSW,** has helped thousands of social workers across the country pass the Association of Social Work Boards (ASWB) examinations associated with all levels of licensure. In recent years, she has consulted in numerous states to assist with establishing licensure test preparation programs.

Dr. Apgar has done research on licensure funded by the American Foundation for Research and Consumer Education in Social Work Regulation and was chairperson of her state's social work licensing board. She is a past president of the New Jersey Chapter of the National Association of Social Workers (NASW) and has been on its National Board of Directors. In 2014, the chapter presented her with a Lifetime Achievement Award. Dr. Apgar has taught in both undergraduate and graduate social work programs and has extensive direct practice, policy, and management experience in the social work field.

# Social Work Licensing Clinical Exam Practice Test

## 170-Question Full-Length Print Practice Test for the ASWB LCSW Exam

Third Edition

Dawn Apgar, PhD, LSW, ACSW

First Springer Publishing edition 2017, subsequent edition 2021



Springer Publishing Company, LLC
902 Carnegie Center/Suite 140, Princeton, NJ 08540
www.springerpub.com
connect.springerpub.com

*Acquisitions Editor*: Cindy Kitchel
*Production Editor*: Susan White
*Compositor*: Thomson Digital

*ISBN*: 978-0-8261-7597-7
*e-book ISBN*: 978-0-8261-5467-5
*DOI*: 10.1891/9780826154675

24 25 26 27 / 5 4 3 2 1



**Library of Congress Control Number: 2024947824**



Printed in the United States of America by Gasch Printing.

*To Bill, Ryan, and Alex*

*You remind me what is important, support me so I can do it all,
and always inspire me to be a better person*

# Contents

# Introduction

Despite social workers' best efforts to study for and pass the Association of Social Work Boards (ASWB) examinations for licensure, they can encounter difficulties answering questions correctly that can ultimately lead to challenges in passing. Social workers who struggle with standardized test taking or have failed the ASWB examinations find themselves at a loss in finding resources to assist them in identifying the mistakes they made and strategies for correcting these errors. The focus of test preparation courses and guides is usually the review of the relevant content and supplying some study and test-taking tips. However, when these resources do not result in passing the ASWB examinations, social workers do not know where to turn for help.

Often, social workers will turn to taking practice tests in an effort to gauge their readiness for the ASWB examinations. In addition, they will try to use them to identify gaps in knowledge and errors in problem-solving that prevent desired outcomes. Such an approach is understandable because there has been a void in available diagnostic resources. However, for several reasons, use of existing practice examinations is not usually helpful.

First, it is difficult to identify specific content that is used by test developers to formulate actual questions. For example, many practice tests do not provide rationales for the correct answer and incorrect response choices. In addition, they usually do not let social workers know which specific ASWB content areas were being tested (e.g., Human Development, Diversity, and Behavior in the Environment; Assessment, Diagnosis, and Treatment Planning; Psychotherapy, Clinical Intervention, and Case Management; or Professional Values and Ethics). The ASWB competencies and corresponding Knowledge, Skills, and Abilities statements (KSAs) that form the basis for question development are also not included. Thus, when questions are answered incorrectly, social workers do not know which knowledge in the ASWB content areas, competencies, and KSAs is lacking so they can go back and review relevant source materials. Along with the correct answers, this practice test provides rationales and the content area, with the KSA in parentheses following the content area.

Based on a practice analysis conducted by the ASWB, which outlines the content to be included on the exam, content areas, competencies, and KSAs are created. Content areas are the broad knowledge areas that are measured by each exam. The content areas structure the content for exam construction and score reporting purposes. When receiving exam scores, failing candidates are given feedback on their performance in each content area of the exam. Competencies describe meaningful sets of abilities that are important to the job of a social worker within each content area. Finally, KSAs structure the content of the exam for item development purposes. The KSAs provide further details about the nature and range of exam content that is included in the competencies. Each KSA describes a discrete knowledge component that is the basis for individual exam questions that may be used to measure the competency.

Having the ASWB content areas and KSAs identified is critical in order to make practice tests useful for diagnosing knowledge weaknesses. The following example illustrates the usefulness of having this material explicitly stated.

## SAMPLE QUESTION

A social worker at a community mental health agency is doing a home visit to a client as he has not gotten his medication refilled as prescribed. The social worker learns that he has not been taking it for several weeks due to a belief that it is not helping alleviate his thought to "just end things." In order to assist the client, the social worker should **FIRST:**

A. Accompany the client to his next appointment with the psychiatrist to see if another medication can be prescribed

B. Explain to the client the importance of taking the medication as prescribed

C. Conduct a suicide risk assessment

## ANSWER

1. **Correct Answer:** C. Conduct a suicide risk assessment

**Rationale:** Social workers have an ethical duty to respect and promote the right of clients to self-determination. However, there are times when social workers' responsibility to the larger society or specific legal obligations supersedes their commitment to respecting clients' decisions or wishes. These instances are when, in the social workers' professional judgment, clients' actions or potential actions pose a serious, foreseeable, and imminent risk to themselves (including the risk of suicide) or others (in general or aimed at identifiable third parties—duty to warn). The client's thoughts to "just end things" may be an indicator of suicide risk. The social worker should FIRST assess the degree of risk that is present to determine whether the client is safe without use of the medication and can wait to discuss his concerns with his psychiatrist at a future appointment or needs to be treated immediately, voluntarily or involuntarily.

**Question Type:** Reasoning

**Content Area:** Assessment, Diagnosis, and Treatment Planning (The indicators and risk factors of the clients/client system's danger to self and others)

If this answer was missed, social workers need the rationale for the correct response choice in order to identify the need to review materials related to assessment, diagnosis, and treatment planning, which is the content area being assessed. Specifically, this question focused on determining competency with regard to identifying indicators of client danger to self or others (KSA). Reviewing the risk factors and signs associated with suicide would be a useful place to start. In addition, refined literature searches on behavioral, emotional, and psychological warning signs would produce more targeted information to fill this information gap.

Most practice tests will not help direct social workers toward these resources as they do not provide the ASWB content areas and KSAs being tested. They also do not give valuable information on the topics as a way for social workers to understand the rationales for the correct answers and why the others are incorrect.

Second, practice tests rarely explicitly identify the test-taking strategies that must be used in order to select the correct answers from the others provided. Even when rationales are provided on practice tests, the test-taking strategies that should be generalized to other questions are often not explicitly stated. This void makes it difficult for social workers to see problems that they may be having in problem solving, outside of content gaps.

For example, in the sample question, social workers must be keenly aware of the client's thoughts to "just end things" as delineated by quotation marks. These thoughts may be an indication of suicide risk.

There is also a qualifying word—FIRST—used, which is bold and capitalized in the question. The use of this qualifying word indicates that more than one of the provided response choices may be correct, but selecting the one that precedes the others is what is being asked. When clients are potentially suicidal, social workers must FIRST assess for risk.

This tool was developed to assist social workers in identifying their knowledge gaps and difficulties in problem-solving by providing critical information including the content area being assessed and the test-taking strategies required in order to answer questions correctly.

Social workers should use this practice test to identify:

- Question wording that is important to selecting correct answers
- Key social work concepts that are being assessed
- Useful problem-solving strategies and themes
- Mistakes in logic
- Content areas and KSAs that require additional study

This test is not intended to be a study guide, but does contain important social work content related to the KSAs. This practice test helps social workers who are struggling to find answers about what mistakes they are making and what they need to study more. It can be used in conjunction with existing study guides that provide an overview of needed social work material, *Social Work Licensing Clinical Exam Guide: Comprehensive ASWB LCSW Exam Review,* Fourth Edition, by this author.

Social workers must understand their learning styles and use available resources to fill in existing content gaps through the use of visual, auditory, and/or hands-on materials. Most social work content is available for little or no cost. There is no need to purchase expensive products as there are many educational materials available for free. However, it is important that social workers make sure that these resources are rooted in the values and knowledge base of the profession, as well as produced by those providing legitimate instruction. There are no tricks or secrets associated with passing the examination that can replace learning and understanding a topic. The application of material requires being able to relate it to various scenarios or vignettes.

# Getting It Right: Understanding Multiple-Choice Tests and Applying Key Social Work Concepts

On the ASWB examinations, social workers often struggle with application and reasoning questions which require them to take what has been learned and use it to identify correct answers given hypothetical contexts. These items require test takers to use logic or reasoning to arrive at the same response choice. Social workers are not prepared for these assessment methods as multiple-choice testing is not frequently used in social work educational programs. Often, test takers are frustrated as they do not know what is being asked in questions and how to choose between response choices that seem similar. Becoming more familiar with the construction of multiple-choice tests, as well as remembering concepts which are hallmarks within the social work profession, can greatly assist.

## MULTIPLE-CHOICE EXAMINATIONS

Many social workers do not have experience taking multiple-choice tests and are unfamiliar with the format of questions. A multiple-choice question is composed of several important parts.

*Stem*—A stem identifies the question or problem. In ASWB examinations, stems are the KSAs or concepts to be assessed. A stem often appears at the end of a question, right before the response choices. It can be a complete or incomplete sentence. A stem tells the test taker the focus of the question and how to apply the background information provided in the question. Often, questions can appear broad, but each is testing a specific KSA which is contained in the stem. The goal is to identify the stem before looking at the response choices. If the stem is clearly understood, selecting the key or correct answer will be easier.

*Key*—A key is the correct answer to the question which is based on content learned in social work educational programs. The ASWB tests assess knowledge so the key is superior to the alternatives based on conceptual information that was learned in school that is not contained in the other response choices.

*Distractors*—Distractors are plausible but incorrect answers to a question. Rarely will response choices appear that can be easily eliminated. The ASWB does not use "all of the above" or "none of the above" response choices. Distractors are similar in length and language to the key or correct answer. Often distractors represent common mistakes made by social workers. Test takers often inappropriately select incorrect response choices or distractors as they feel that they incorporate or overlap correct ones. Each response choice must be assessed based on the explicit wording used and social workers must not assume redundancy between response choices.

The following example will assist with identifying the parts of a sample multiple-choice question:

A client states that he has received services in the past and "it did not work out." He appears tense and angry, telling the social worker that he does not want the social worker to speak with his prior provider. In order to best assist the client, the social worker should **FIRST**:

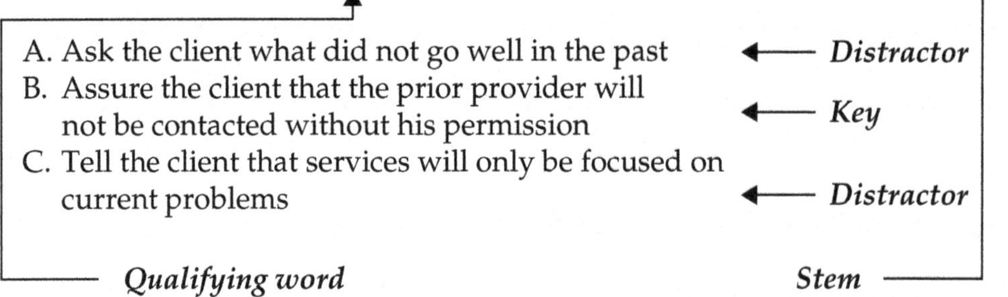


This question asks the best action to "assist" the client. The goal is to help the client. The first sentence in an ASWB vignette is often the presenting problem. In this scenario, the client is no longer receiving services from a prior provider, though the reason for the termination is unknown. The second sentence describes his current emotions, which are tense and angry, as well as his desire not to have the social worker speak to the prior provider. The stem requires the test taker to select an answer that is most helpful when confronted with an emotional client who is guarded about his past. There is a qualifying word—FIRST—which indicates that the order of these responses is important. A qualifying word may appear in or near stems of questions and should be closely attended to as they contain vital information for distinguishing between keys and distractors.

Social workers must first calm a client before asking questions. Telling the client that services will only be focused on current problems does not address the emotional state of a client. Clearly, his prior experience with service delivery is impacting his affect and behavior during this initial meeting. Assuring him that he has the right to make decisions about his treatment will assist with engagement, which is essential for the development of a helping relationship.

## APPLYING KEY SOCIAL WORK CONCEPTS

There are many KSAs tested on the licensure examinations. It is very important for test takers to be familiar with the topics that will be assessed. While there are many specific KSAs, there are some important social work concepts that transcend all of them. These are principles that must be considered when distinguishing the key from distractors. While not exhaustive, these themes are consistent across questions and can be used to assist with identifying correct answers. However, the degree to which each is relevant to a particular question varies. A question to help with test taking is listed after each relevant concept.

Social workers have groups, organizations, and communities as clients.

- *Does the question specifically identify an individual or family as the client or could the level of intervention be bigger (the client is a group, an organization, and/or a community)?*
  - Social workers do all types of intervention including provision of concrete services, case management, policy practice, and community organization.
- *Does the question explicitly state the type of service being provided? If not, the KSA is universal across intervention types.*
  - Social workers respect client self-determination.
- *Does the answer respect the client's right to make decisions?*
  - Social workers are trained to identify the root causes of problems.
- *Does the answer address the systematic issues rather than those impacted?*
  - Social workers engage collaboratively with clients.
- *Does the answer mention the client implicitly or explicitly as opposed to just the social worker?*
  - Social workers use a systems approach to understanding functioning.

- *Does the answer consider the interplay between biopsychosocial-cultural-spiritual functioning or the micro, mezzo, and macro levels of intervention?*
    - Social workers apply their knowledge in diverse settings and with many populations.
- *Does the answer reflect knowledge that can be generalized to all agencies, methods of practice, and client groups?*
    - Social workers are committed to social justice and working with those who are oppressed.
- *Does the answer ensure equal rights, especially for those who are poor and/or marginalized?*
    - Simply enhancing knowledge about multiple-choice question formatting and keeping key social work concepts in mind can greatly enhance performance. Armed with this information, test takers are ready to take a full-length practice test to identify any further problems which may be present and can interfere with passing.

# Recommendations for Using This Practice Test

Actual ASWB test results are based on 150 scored items and an additional 20 questions that are not scored because they are being piloted. These pilot items are intermixed with the scored ones and not distinguished in any way. Social workers never find out which ones are scored and which questions are being piloted.

In an effort to make this practice test as similar to the examination as possible, it contains 170 questions, the same number as the actual exam, proportionately distributed within the four domains—Human Development, Diversity, and Behavior in the Environment (41 questions); Assessment, Diagnosis, and Treatment Planning (51 questions); Psychotherapy, Clinical Interventions, and Case Management (46 questions); and Professional Values and Ethics (32 questions). These proportions mirror the distribution of questions across these domains on the actual ASWB examination.

The best way for social workers to use this practice test is to:

- Complete it after you have studied yet are still feeling uncertain about problem areas
- Finish it completely during a 4-hour block of time as a way of gauging fatigue and length of time it will take to complete the actual examination
- Avoid looking up the answers until after you have finished completely
- Generate a listing of content areas in which you have experienced problems and use it as the basis of a study plan employing other source materials to further review the concepts
- Generalize the test-taking strategies for future use on the actual examination

This practice test is to be used as a diagnostic tool, so social workers should not worry about getting incorrect answers but should view them as learning opportunities to avoid common pitfalls and pinpoint learning needs. On the actual ASWB examination, the number of questions that social workers need to correctly answer generally varies from 90 to 107 of the 150 scored items. Since this practice test is 170 items, 20 questions would need to be randomly removed to determine if the overall number correct falls into this range.[1] Since many social workers who do not pass find themselves "just missing" these pass points, the value of identifying content gaps and difficulties in problem solving is tremendous because it can result in additional correct answers on the actual test.

[1] Because different test takers receive different questions, raw scores on the actual exam—the actual number of correctly answered questions—go through an "equating process" to make sure that those receiving more difficult questions are not placed at a disadvantage. Equating adjusts the number of items needed to answer correctly up or down depending on the difficulty levels. This practice test has not gone through the equating process, which is why the number of correct answers needed to "pass" using ASWB standards cannot be determined.

# Pass Guarantee

If you use this resource to prepare for your exam and do not pass, you may return it for a refund of your full purchase price, excluding tax, shipping, and handling. To receive a refund, return your product along with a copy of your exam score report and original receipt showing purchase of new product (not used). Product must be returned and received within 180 days of the original purchase date. Refunds will be issued within 8 weeks from acceptance and approval. One offer per person and address. This offer is valid for U.S. residents only. Void where prohibited. To initiate a refund, please contact Customer Service at csexamprep@springerpub.com.

# 170-Question Full-Length Exam

1. Which of the following **BEST** describes the difference between obsessive-compulsive disorder (OCD) and obsessive-compulsive personality disorder (OCPD)?

   **A.** OCD focuses on order and control, while OCPD involves obsessions and compulsions.

   **B.** OCD is treatable with therapy, while OCPD can be managed but is part of the personality

   **C.** OCD is distressing for the individual with the condition, whereas OCPD is problematic for others.

2. A social worker is working with an older adult client who recently moved into an assisted living facility after the death of their spouse. The client has expressed feelings of loneliness and struggles to adjust to the new environment. In order to improve the client's quality of life, the social worker should:

   **A.** Encourage the client to participate in social activities offered by the facility

   **B.** Help the client to focus on accepting the loss of the spouse

   **C.** Assist the client in setting up regular visits with family members and friends

3. A social worker learns that a client is engaging in self-cutting behavior. Which of the following is **MOST** likely the cause of this behavior?

   **A.** Desire to gain attention from others

   **B.** Response to feeling disconnected from social relationships

   **C.** Attempt to manage intense emotional pain and distress

4. A social worker is providing therapy to a woman and her teenage child individually after a traumatic accident that resulted in the death of other family members. During the individual therapy sessions, the woman and child each describe an emotional distancing between them due to communication difficulties and frequent arguments. To **BEST** assist these clients, the social worker should:

   **A.** Provide suggestions during individual therapy for productive interaction opportunities

   **B.** Engage in conjoint sessions to work on communication and conflict resolution

   **C.** Refer the clients to a relationship support group to connect with others facing similar challenges

5. A social worker is treating a client with borderline personality disorder (BPD). The client has severed relationships with family and recently quit a job despite financial instability. When using a dialectical behavior therapy approach, which of the following should the social worker focus on **FIRST**?

   **A.** Helping the client build relationships with family members who can act as supports

   **B.** Assisting the client in finding employment to avoid financial crisis

   **C.** Helping the client recognize and label personal emotions properly

6. A social worker is assessing a child who reports experiencing mood swings over the past year. The client describes having several episodes of elevated mood and increased energy lasting a few days, followed by periods of depressive symptoms lasting for a couple of weeks. The client's symptoms do not reach the severity of full-blown mania or major depression but are noticeable and persistent. Based on this description, which diagnosis is the **MOST** accurate for this client?

   **A.** Bipolar I disorder

   **B.** Bipolar II disorder

   **C.** Cyclothymic disorder

**7.** A social worker is evaluating a client who exhibits physical symptoms without a clear medical cause. The client's primary concern is obtaining financial compensation and avoiding responsibilities. Which of the following **BEST** describes the client's condition?

**A.** Malingering

**B.** Somatization

**C.** Sublimation

**8.** A social worker is working with a client who has been struggling with severe anxiety and depression following the recent death of a close family member. The client has been unable to maintain regular employment, has withdrawn from social activities, and reports persistent feelings of hopelessness. Additionally, the client has a history of substance abuse and is currently on medication for managing anxiety. During sessions, the client expresses ambivalence about seeking additional support and shows reluctance to engage in therapy. In order to assist, the social worker should **FIRST**:

**A.** Discuss the issues that have prevented treatment in the past

**B.** Determine the root cause of the anxiety and depression

**C.** Identify a small step that the client can take toward goal achievement

**9.** A social worker is assessing an 8-year-old child who has been experiencing intense, frequent outbursts when experiencing minor conflicts. These outbursts, along with a persistently irritable and angry mood, have been ongoing for more than a year. Which of the following is **MOST** likely the diagnosis for this child?

**A.** Disruptive mood dysregulation disorder (DMDD)

**B.** Conduct disorder

**C.** Oppositional defiant disorder (ODD)

**10.** A social worker is working with a client who has been diagnosed with major depressive disorder (MDD). The client reports persistent feelings of sadness, loss of interest in daily activities, and significant difficulty concentrating. Which of the following medications is the client **MOST** likely prescribed for these symptoms?

**A.** Risperidone (Risperdal)

**B.** Sertraline (Zoloft)

**C.** Diazepam (Valium)

11. A client who is undergoing treatment for a chronic health condition reports persistent fatigue and difficulty concentrating, and a recent blood test indicates elevated levels of a specific blood marker. Which of the following should the social worker consider the **MOST** important concern?

**A.** Social and emotional effects of the health condition

**B.** Elevated blood marker results

**C.** Self-care regimen which includes proper rest

12. A social worker is working with a client who has been diagnosed with borderline personality disorder (BPD). Which of the following behaviors is the social worker **MOST** likely to observe in the client?

**A.** Fear of abandonment

**B.** Compulsive adherence to rules

**C.** Grandiosity of self

13. A social worker learns that a client's Thematic Apperception Test (TAT) reveals themes of abandonment, rejection, and distrust. Which of the following is **MOST** likely the client diagnosis based on these themes?

**A.** Paranoia

**B.** Borderline personality disorder

**C.** Avoidant personality disorder

14. Which of the following is the **MOST** important motivator for both factitious disorder imposed on self (FDIS) and factitious disorder imposed on another (FDIA)?

**A.** Sympathy and attention

**B.** External rewards or incentives

**C.** Fear of abandonment

15. A social worker meets with a client who has recently been hospitalized for unexplained physical symptoms, including difficulty walking. No medical causes have been found for these difficulties which coincide with the client accepting a new job that is extremely stressful. Which of the following defense mechanisms is **MOST** likely the cause of these ailments?

**A.** Repression

**B.** Conversion

**C.** Displacement

**16.** A social worker is meeting with a client who has recently started a new job with significant stress due to work-related issues. The client reports that "everything is going well" but the client has increased headaches and stomachaches. A medical evaluation shows no underlying physical causes for these symptoms. Which defense mechanism is **MOST** likely being utilized by the client?

**A.** Projection

**B.** Conversion

**C.** Denial

**17.** Which of the following **BEST** describes when social workers should review confidentiality information including limits and mandates for reporting?

**A.** Prior to the first meeting

**B.** During the engagement process

**C.** Throughout the helping process

**18.** A social worker receives a court order for client information that the social worker feels is harmful to the client if released. The client has not consented to the release. In order to address the situation ethically, the social worker should:

**A.** Release the information to the court as the social worker is legally required to do so

**B.** Request that the court withdraw or limit the order

**C.** Refuse to release the information

**19.** A social worker notices an error in a case note that was written and placed in a client's file. In order to address this situation ethically, the social worker should **NEXT**:

**A.** Replace the original note in the file with one that corrects the error

**B.** Add an addendum to the original note that includes an explanation of the error

**C.** Seek supervision or consultation in order to comply with agency policy in this situation

20. A social worker is treating a client with schizoid personality disorder. The social worker learns that the client has few interpersonal relationships. Which of the following is **MOST** likely the reason for this isolation?

**A.** Preference for solitude

**B.** Bizarre and odd behavior

**C.** Pervasive distrust of others

21. A social worker is assessing a client with treatment-resistant schizophrenia who has been prescribed Clozaril (clozapine). The client exhibits behaviors such as severe agitation, aggression, and persistent suicidal ideation despite previous treatments. Which of the following would a social worker **MOST** need to monitor as part of this client's medication management protocols?

**A.** Risk of developing serious infections

**B.** Weight loss resulting in malnutrition

**C.** Excessive salivation leading to dehydration

22. A social worker is working with a client who has recently gone through a traumatic event but is unable to recall details of the event. The client insists that the event was not as serious as it actually was. The client has difficulty discussing the event and shows a lack of emotional response when the event is mentioned. Which defense mechanism is the client **MOST** likely using?

**A.** Repression

**B.** Denial

**C.** Reaction formation

23. A social worker is nearing the end of a therapeutic relationship with a client who has made significant progress in addressing anxiety and improving daily functioning. The client reports feeling more confident and has successfully applied coping strategies in daily life. In order to ensure that the client is prepared for termination, the social worker should **NEXT**:

**A.** Summarize progress and future needs with the client

**B.** Review with the client the coping skills currently being employed

**C.** Identify community-based supports that can assist with aftercare

**24.** Which model of addiction describes that substance use helps cope with underlying psychological or emotional issues?

**A.** Disease model

**B.** Family model

**C.** Self-medication model

**25.** A social worker is preparing to conduct a research study involving human subjects to evaluate the effectiveness of a new community support program on improving mental health outcomes. The study will involve interviews and surveys with participants who are currently receiving services from the program. To ensure the research is conducted ethically, the social worker should:

**A.** Develop a detailed research proposal outlining the study's objectives, methodology, and potential risks to be reviewed by an Institutional Review Board (IRB)

**B.** Obtain informed consent from all participants, ensuring they fully understand the purpose of the study, the procedures involved, potential risks, and their right to withdraw at any time

**C.** Secure funding and resources needed to conduct the research, including staff support, data collection tools, and participant incentives, to ensure the study's success

**26.** A social worker is working with a client who is preparing to transition from intensive therapy to a less frequent maintenance phase. The client has made significant progress but needs to continue practicing new skills and managing challenges independently. To ensure a smooth transition, the social worker should **NEXT**:

**A.** Establish a contract with the client for the next phase of treatment

**B.** Discuss the client's feelings about reducing the level of service

**C.** Monitor the client's progress to ensure that the progress made is maintained

**27.** A social worker is meeting with a client who is struggling with the emotional impact of being laid off from a job, a situation that has caused the client significant stress and feelings of inadequacy. The social worker has previously experienced a similar job loss and found ways to cope with the situation. The social worker is considering whether to share personal experiences with the client to provide support. Which of the following is the **MOST** important consideration for the social worker in deciding whether to disclose this information?

**A.** Potential to build rapport by sharing a personal story of overcoming similar challenges

**B.** Need to ensure that sharing the experience will not distract the client from addressing personal needs

**C.** Usefulness of the personal experience to provide specific solutions for the client in handling the current job loss

**28.** A social worker is beginning to work with a new client who has been referred for assistance with managing chronic stress and improving coping skills. The client is hesitant about starting therapy and has expressed concerns about confidentiality and the effectiveness of the process. To effectively engage the client, the social worker should **FIRST**:

**A.** Discuss what the client can expect as part of the helping process

**B.** Outline some of the potential goals and specific interventions available

**C.** Ask the client why there was a desire to seek treatment

**29.** A social worker is working with a client who has a history of housing instability. The social worker learns that the client is planning to make a decision that the social worker believes will likely lead to homelessness again. The social worker is concerned about the potential negative impact of this decision on the client's stability. In this situation, the social worker should **NEXT**:

**A.** Educate the client that the decision is not advised so that the client can reconsider

**B.** Explore the client's reasoning for the decision

**C.** Help the client identify alternative courses of action that may prevent homelessness

**30.** A social worker is working with a client who frequently arrives late to sessions and consistently brings up new issues during the last few minutes of each appointment, making it difficult to end on time. In order to address this behavior, the social worker should:

**A.** Clarify the session start and end times and emphasize the importance of punctuality

**B.** Schedule shorter sessions to minimize the impact of the client's lateness

**C.** Reschedule the appointments to a different time of day when the client is likely to be on time

**31.** A social work supervisor observes that a supervisee struggles with maintaining professional boundaries during emotionally charged client interactions. To help the supervisee develop these skills, the supervisor should:

**A.** Conduct a training session on boundary setting

**B.** Role model appropriate boundary-setting behaviors during client interactions

**C.** Assign readings on managing client emotions and boundaries

**32.** A social worker is providing support to an older adult client who is in the advanced stages of a terminal illness. The client expresses a strong desire to make decisions regarding end-of-life care, including the choice of hospice services and the extent of medical interventions. The client's family, however, is concerned that the client's choices might not be in the client's best interest and prefers a more aggressive treatment approach. In this situation, the social worker should:

**A.** Advocate for the client's preferences even if they conflict with the family's wishes

**B.** Encourage the client to reconsider choices in light of the family's preferences

**C.** Facilitate a family meeting to discuss the client's wishes to mediate a compromise

**33.** A social work supervisor is considering different models of supervision to address various needs of staff. The supervisor is particularly focused on discussing challenging clients, giving professional feedback, and identifying areas for improvement. Which model of supervision would be **MOST** appropriate?

**A.** Peer supervision

**B.** Individual supervision

**C.** Group supervision

**34.** Which of the following describes why individuals are more likely to overdose when relapsing while in recovery from substance use disorders?

**A.** Decreased tolerance levels

**B.** Increased potency of substances

**C.** Presence of more lethal substances

**35.** A social worker is assessing a client who presents with symptoms of both substance use disorder and a mental health condition. To effectively assess whether there are co-occurring disorders, the social worker should **FIRST**:

**A.** Help the client abstain from the substance so that the social worker can determine whether the mental health symptoms persist

**B.** Collect detailed information from the client to identify the chronicity and severity of behaviors and symptoms

**C.** Rule out the existence of a substance use disorder using diagnostic criteria to focus on mental health issues

**36.** A social worker is preparing for an upcoming supervision session with a supervisor. To **BEST** plan for the meeting, the social work should:

**A.** Reflect on any challenges or successes since the last supervision session

**B.** Identify questions about agency policies which are unclear or problematic

**C.** Prepare a list of goals and issues related to current work requirements

**37.** A social worker is assisting the family of a client who has recently been denied admission to a nursing home. The client, an older adult with multiple chronic health conditions, requires substantial support for daily activities and medical care. After reviewing the denial letter, the social worker learns that the decision was based on the level of care determination. Which of the following is **MOST** likely the factor that contributed to the decision to deny admission?

**A.** Inability to perform activities of daily living

**B.** Need for advanced medical treatments

**C.** Staff shortages that prevent meeting the client's needs at this time

38. A social worker is working with a client who is experiencing delirium tremens (DTs) as a result of alcohol withdrawal. Which of the following treatments is the client **MOST** likely to receive to assist with this issue?

**A.** Medication to manage symptoms

**B.** Therapy to assist with cravings

**C.** Environmental restrictions to prevent access to alcohol

39. A social worker has been offered a job that requires licensure to provide services legally. In order to ensure eligibility to obtain the necessary license, the social worker should:

**A.** Review the licensure regulations in the jurisdiction

**B.** Consult with the human resource department of the hiring agency

**C.** Contact the professional social work association for consultation

40. A social worker is working with a client who has experienced a series of issues, including difficulties in both school performance and social interactions. The client's problems seem to have different origins, but all result in similar negative outcomes. Which of the following concepts **BEST** defines this situation?

**A.** Negative entropy

**B.** Homeostasis

**C.** Equifinality

41. A social worker observes interactions in a family in which the roles and expectations of family members are not aligning. For example, a child is expected to take on responsibilities that are developmentally inappropriate, while a parent is not fulfilling a caregiving role effectively. Which of the following **BEST** describes this role issue?

**A.** Role confusion

**B.** Role discomplementarity

**C.** Role strain

**42.** A social worker is observing a group of 4-year-old children playing together. A child insists that a toy truck can talk and becomes very upset when others do not share this belief. This child also struggles to understand that the toy truck cannot be in two places at once. Which stage of cognitive development is this child **MOST** likely in?

**A.** Formal operational

**B.** Preoperational

**C.** Concrete operational

**43.** A social worker is assisting a client who has recently arrived in the country as a refugee. The client's issues include cultural adjustment, legal issues, and fiscal stability. Which of the following should be a primary consideration when locating services?

**A.** Social service eligibility considering the refugee status

**B.** Trauma-informed care availability given psychological distress suffered

**C.** Discrimination due to xenophobia

**44.** A school social worker is called to intervene in a conflict between two students who have been arguing and disrupting the lesson. The teacher reports that the students have a history of not getting along, and the tension has escalated to the point of affecting the entire class. To help resolve the conflict, the social worker should **FIRST**:

**A.** Meet with each student individually to understand unique perspectives on the conflict

**B.** Facilitate a joint meeting with both students to encourage open dialogue

**C.** Develop a classroom management plan with the teacher that addresses disruptive behavior

**45.** A social worker discovers that a client is also a neighbor and attends the same community events as the social worker. To manage this dual relationship effectively, the social worker should:

**A.** Discuss ways to resolve the conflicts with the client

**B.** Avoid acknowledging the client in the neighborhood or at community events

**C.** Discontinue attending community events to prevent unnecessary contact

**46.** A social work supervisor notices that a supervisee is struggling with a client who displays extreme dependency and seeks constant reassurance. During supervision, the supervisee exhibits similar behaviors, such as seeking excessive validation and showing defensiveness. In order to manage this issue, the social work supervisor should:

**A.** Discuss how the supervisee's client dynamics might be influencing behavior in supervision

**B.** Focus on the supervisee's client work to help resolve the parallel supervisory dynamics

**C.** Suggest the supervisee seek outside support for the client issues to avoid a conflict of interest

**47.** A social worker feels strong disagreement with many decisions made by an interdisciplinary treatment team of which the social worker is a member. The social worker is becoming increasingly frustrated by this disagreement, with these feelings starting to impact client care. In order to appropriately address this situation, the social worker should **FIRST**:

**A.** Reflect on how professional values and beliefs might be influencing perspectives and interactions within the team

**B.** Express these feelings of frustration to team members so that they can be appropriately processed and resolved

**C.** Seek supervision or consultation to identify ways in which the social worker can be more assertive in team decision-making

**48.** During a peer supervision session, a social worker notices that the group is quickly converging on a single approach to a challenging client situation. The social worker is concerned that this convergence might be a result of groupthink rather than a thorough evaluation of all options. To **BEST** address this concern, the social worker should:

**A.** Gather additional information to determine if this issue is persistent in all discussions

**B.** Agree with the group as there should be unanimity of opinions in peer supervision

**C.** Encourage the group to explore alternative approaches and critically evaluate each option

**49.** A social worker employed by an agency is preparing for a home visit with a client who has a history of aggression. In order to take necessary safety precautions for the visit, the social worker should:

**A.** Ensure that the address of the visit is properly noted on the social worker's agency schedule

**B.** Suggest meeting the client in a public space to ensure a more controlled environment

**C.** Arrange to check in with a supervisor or colleague before and after the visit

**50.** A social worker is working with an adolescent who is greatly influenced by peer pressure. The youth does well in school as he follows the behavioral actions and norms of others. Which level of moral reasoning is **MOST** likely represented by this behavior?

**A.** Preconventional

**B.** Postconventional

**C.** Conventional

**51.** A social worker notices that a client often becomes quiet and withdraws during discussions about difficult topics. Using nonverbal communication to help the client feel more comfortable and engaged, the social worker should:

**A.** Maintain consistent eye contact to show attentiveness and support

**B.** Lean forward slightly to convey interest and empathy

**C.** Nod occasionally to encourage the client to continue speaking

**52.** A social worker is preparing to discharge a client from a residential treatment facility. The client has made significant progress but still faces challenges in managing a condition. Which of the following is the **MOST** important part of the discharge process?

**A.** Providing the client with a comprehensive list of community resources

**B.** Ensuring the client has a clear understanding of the protocols needed for managing the condition

**C.** Reviewing progress and anticipating future needs based on the prognosis

**53.** Which of the following examples **BEST** represents positive punishment of a child?

A. Removing a child's toy for not completing homework

B. Giving extra chores to a child who broke a rule

C. Ignoring a child's bad behavior to reduce its occurrence

**54.** A social worker is providing feedback to a client who is not demonstrating appropriate progress in a psychoeducational class. The client has struggled to apply the skills and concepts taught and seems discouraged. To **BEST** assist the client, the social worker should:

A. Suggest that the client revisit previous lessons to reinforce concepts

B. Highlight the client's efforts and progress to date

C. Identify realistic goals for improvement which include more opportunities for practice

**55.** The **PRIMARY** purpose of biofeedback in therapeutic settings is to:

A. Provide a baseline for psychological stress

B. Increase client awareness and control of physiological functions

C. Understand the interplay between physical and psychological processes

**56.** A social worker is meeting with a new client who experienced a house fire that resulted in homelessness and a state of acute emotional distress. The client is struggling to manage immediate emotional reactions and is feeling overwhelmed by the loss. In order to help in this situation, the social worker should:

A. Assist the client in setting goals for the future to help the client move forward after the crisis

B. Provide immediate support to address the client's housing and financial needs

C. Conduct an assessment of the client's past trauma and its impact on the current emotional state

**57.** A social worker is working with a client who has difficulty managing anger and is looking for effective ways to teach anger management techniques. In order to **BEST** assist, the social worker should:

A. Practice specific anger management techniques together during meetings

B. Refer the client to an anger management support group to facilitate learning from others' experiences

C. Encourage the client to journal to identify patterns and triggers over time

**58.** A social worker is working with a client who has recently experienced multiple crises, including the loss of a job, a recent breakup, and severe financial difficulties. The client reports feeling overwhelmed, having trouble sleeping, and housing instability. The client also mentions feeling isolated from a support network. In this situation, the social worker should **FIRST:**

**A.** Refer the client to emergency assistance to provide financial stability

**B.** Explore the client's coping skills to ensure resilience during this time of crisis

**C.** Conduct a safety assessment to ensure the client's well-being

**59.** A social worker is conducting a risk assessment for a client with a history of self-harm and substance abuse. Which of the following is the **MOST** important aspect of the risk assessment process to guide immediate intervention by the social worker?

**A.** Identifying dynamic risk factors

**B.** Increasing knowledge about static risk factors

**C.** Knowing the available community-based crisis resources

**60.** A social worker is developing a plan for an older adult client who is experiencing difficulties with aging, including health issues, decreased mobility, and social isolation. When planning, the social worker should set goals with the client to:

**A.** Manage medical treatments

**B.** Enhance social relationships

**C.** Encourage self-determination

**61.** A social worker is working with a client who feels disempowered and lacks confidence in the ability to make changes that impact the future. In order to **BEST** empower the client, the social worker should:

**A.** Help the client set short-term, achievable goals to build confidence and decision-making skills

**B.** Assist the client to understand that the future is guided by current acts to improve the situation

**C.** Facilitate the client's participation in an advocacy group to become a change agent

62. When a social worker is partializing a problem to help a client address it more effectively, the social worker should **FIRST**:

**A.** Assess the client's readiness to tackle each component of the problem

**B.** Review the client's past experiences and coping strategies related to similar issues

**C.** Identify and prioritize the smaller, manageable components of the problem

63. A social worker is working with a client who struggles with a negative body image. The client frequently expresses dissatisfaction with appearance and reports that these feelings are affecting daily life and relationships. In order to **BEST** assist, the social worker should:

**A.** Help the client to understand that physical appearance should not be judged

**B.** Explore with the client how negative beliefs about body image are linked to self-esteem

**C.** Assure the client that many people have similar irrational insecurities

64. A social worker is working with a client who has a history of substance use and has recently expressed interest in making a change. To effectively support the client, the social worker should **FIRST**:

**A.** Conduct a motivational interviewing session with the client

**B.** Refer the client to a support group with others in recovery

**C.** Ask the client to see a physician to assess any medical issues related to the abuse

65. A social worker provides services to a couple who are going through a highly contentious divorce. After termination, the social worker receives a subpoena from one party requesting confidential information as part of a legal proceeding. To handle this situation ethically, the social worker should:

**A.** Comply with the subpoena by providing the requested information to the court

**B.** Inform both parties about the subpoena and consult with legal counsel

**C.** Maintain client confidentiality by claiming privilege

**66.** A social worker is working with a client who is experiencing problems, including family conflict, job stress, and difficulties with community resources. The client is also struggling with personal health issues and feels overwhelmed. Using an ecological perspective, the social worker should:

**A.** Address the client's health issues as they are the most immediate concern

**B.** Explore how the client's environment and family dynamics impact overall well-being

**C.** Help the client prioritize concerns that are related to the client's situation

**67.** A social worker is working with a 10-year-old client who has been experiencing difficulties in school, including frequent outbursts, difficulty following instructions, and struggles with peer relationships. The client's parents report that they are overwhelmed and unsure of how to manage the child's behavior at home. The client also exhibits signs of anxiety, such as excessive worry and avoidance of certain activities. In order to **BEST** assist, the social worker should:

**A.** Engage the family in therapy to address the underlying impact of the child's behavior on interpersonal dynamics

**B.** Implement a behavior management plan to help the child manage the disruptive behaviors

**C.** Provide psychoeducation to the parents about anxiety and strategies for supporting the client

**68.** A social worker using a strategic family therapy approach is working with a family in which the parents are frustrated with their adolescent's defiant behavior and frequent arguments at home. To address the issue, the social worker gives a paradoxical directive, suggesting that the parents intentionally encourage the adolescent to argue more and act out. The social worker is **MOST** likely using this strategy to:

**A.** Help the adolescent feel empowered by allowing the adolescent more control in the family dynamic

**B.** Disrupt the current dysfunctional patterns to encourage the family to think about the adolescent's behavior differently

**C.** Decrease the frequency of arguments by giving the adolescent a structured way to express frustrations

**69.** A social worker is involved in permanency planning for a child in the foster care system who has been in multiple temporary placements due to behavioral issues. Which of the following social work actions is **MOST** important in this process?

**A.** Coordinating with the child's teachers to monitor academic progress and address any issues

**B.** Facilitating meetings between the child and potential adoptive or permanent guardians to assess suitability

**C.** Developing and implementing a behavioral intervention plan to address the child's behavioral challenges

**70.** A social worker employed in an agency is contacted by a former client who asks for help with a new issue that is unrelated to the previous treatment. The social worker is unsure whether it is appropriate to provide assistance due to the past therapeutic relationship. To handle this situation ethically, the social worker should:

**A.** Schedule a time to speak with the client to determine the nature of the existing problem

**B.** Suggest the former client find another provider to avoid any potential conflicts

**C.** Consult agency policy with regard to the appropriateness of serving the former client

**71.** A social worker receives a referral for a family who is seeking assistance with a specific problem that aligns with the social worker's area of expertise. The referral source indicates that new providers are paid incentive payments after serving families for 30 days. To address this situation ethically, the social worker should:

**A.** Accept the referral as the family's needs can be addressed by the social worker

**B.** Decline the referral as incentive payments are not allowed

**C.** Agree to meet with the family before making a decision

72. A social worker is aware that a colleague is frequently late for client appointments and not documenting sessions accurately. The social worker learns that this behavior began when the colleague began caring for an aging parent. To address this situation ethically, the social worker should **FIRST**:

   **A.** Confront the colleague directly about the behavior so that remedial action can be taken

   **B.** Report the colleague's behavior to a supervisor to ensure that clients are not harmed

   **C.** Provide resources about older adult care to the colleague to assist with remedying the situation

73. A social worker is meeting with a client who is struggling with caring for a parent and several small children. The client has recently experienced a job loss and ongoing health issues which have resulted in feelings of frustration and inadequacy. Using a strength-based approach, the social worker should:

   **A.** Help the client identify past successes which have resulted in resilience

   **B.** Explore the specific reasons for the feelings of frustration and inadequacy

   **C.** Obtain respite and other supportive services for the client to assist with current demands

74. Which of the following **BEST** demonstrates congruence in communication by a client?

   **A.** Client smiles while expressing feelings of happiness during a session.

   **B.** Client maintains a neutral tone while discussing an accomplishment.

   **C.** Client avoids eye contact when describing an incident that involved a breach of trust.

75. A social worker is beginning work with a new client who is experiencing difficulties in maintaining employment and relationships. To effectively engage in problem formulation, the social worker should **FIRST**:

   **A.** Praise the client for seeking help for the concerns

   **B.** Clarify the client's presenting problem

   **C.** Focus on solutions rather than difficulties that the client is experiencing

**76.** Which of the following **BEST** describes social work standards with regard to internet searching for client information without informed consent?

**A.** Social workers should conduct internet searches only when it is essential to client safety.

**B.** Social workers should do internet searches to gather any available information about clients.

**C.** Social workers should never use internet searches to gather client information.

**77.** A social worker is working with a client who has been struggling with severe anxiety and has difficulty maintaining consistent employment. The social worker decides to consult with the client's spouse and employer. The spouse reports ongoing conflicts and stress related to the client's symptoms, while the employer notes frequent absences and performance issues. The social worker **MOST** likely used collateral informants in the assessment to:

**A.** Validate the client's self-reported symptoms with external observations

**B.** Gain a clearer understanding of the client's challenges

**C.** Determine the strength of the client's current support systems

**78.** A social worker is helping a client who is struggling with stress and anxiety in daily life. The social worker encourages the client to focus on the present moment and increase awareness of thoughts and feelings as a way of not getting overwhelmed. Which of the following techniques is the social worker employing with this client?

**A.** Cognitive restructuring

**B.** Mindfulness

**C.** Relaxation exercises

**79.** A social worker is meeting with a client who has recently been diagnosed with a chronic illness. The client is experiencing emotional distress, changes in daily functioning, and concerns about the long-term prognosis. In this situation, which of the following should the social worker focus on **FIRST**?

**A.** Management of the physical illness

**B.** Presence of coping skills and available supports

**C.** Impact of the illness on biopsychosocial functioning

80. A social worker is working with a client who has experienced years of discrimination in employment and education. Which of the following impacts is the client **MOST** likely to experience?

A. Reduced social integration

B. Lower economic mobility

C. Heightened mental health issues

81. A client exhibits behaviors that are seen as defensive and often reacts to situations with an inflated sense of self-importance. According to ego psychology, which of the following is **MOST** relevant to understanding this client's behavior?

A. Unresolved unconscious conflicts

B. Conscious self-concept and self-esteem

C. Early childhood experiences with primary caregivers

82. When performing case management, which of the following social work roles is **MOST** effective for assisting clients?

A. Advocate

B. Broker

C. Mediator

83. A social worker is collaborating with a community organization to address systematic discrimination affecting access to housing and employment opportunities. The community has identified several barriers that perpetuate inequality. In order to assist, the social worker should **FIRST**:

A. Develop legal advocacy services to help those negatively affected by this discrimination

B. Advocate for policy changes and reforms for contributing systemic barriers

C. Help the community prioritize policies and practices that are inherently biased

84. A social worker is assessing a client who reports experiencing hematuria, apathy, and lack of job stability. When doing an assessment, which problem should the social worker focus on **FIRST**?

A. Hematuria

B. Job instability

C. Apathy

**85.** A social worker is working with an impoverished community facing challenges such as inadequate housing, limited access to healthcare, and unemployment. Which of the following is **MOST** likely the cause of these issues?

**A.** Increased gentrification that forced economic decline

**B.** Systemic economic disparities that served as institutional barriers

**C.** Lack of engagement that resulted in community disengagement

**86.** A social worker is tasked with evaluating a new social policy designed to improve access to healthcare for underserved communities. Which of the following activities is **MOST** important for the social worker to engage in when conducting the analysis?

**A.** Speaking directly to community members to hear their experiences with the policy

**B.** Examining utilization rates of both inpatient and outpatient healthcare providers

**C.** Ensuring that economic and social access are considered in the analysis

**87.** A social worker is working in a neighborhood that has been experiencing increasing levels of crime and a decline in public services. The social worker is tasked with improving the quality of life of residents. To mobilize community participation, the social worker should **FIRST**:

**A.** Organize town hall meetings so residents can voice their concerns and propose solutions

**B.** Develop a survey to collect resident opinions and priorities regarding neighborhood issues

**C.** Form a coalition of residents to lead initiatives and advocate for policy changes

**88.** A social worker receives a referral for a client in need of subsidized housing. In order to determine eligibility, which of the following would be **MOST** helpful?

**A.** Mental status examination

**B.** Biopsychosocial assessment

**C.** Means testing

**89.** During a group therapy session facilitated by a social worker, the members initially appear distant and hesitant to engage with one another. The social worker aims to strengthen group cohesion to enhance the effectiveness of the intervention. To **BEST** achieve this aim, the social worker should:

**A.** Review group goals with the members

**B.** Encourage members to do more sharing in sessions

**C.** Ask the group to evaluate its interconnected relationships

**90.** A social worker supporting a client who is transitioning to another gender discovers that the client is experiencing complex emotions and practical challenges. To assist the client during this process, the social worker should:

**A.** Provide information on the effects of medical procedures and treatments

**B.** Help the client to further explore both gender identity and expression

**C.** Serve as a support broker for the client during the process

**91.** Which of the following is **MOST** important when a social worker is providing services to a client who is transitioning to another gender?

**A.** Knowledge about gender-affirming medical interventions and treatments

**B.** Provision of a supportive environment that respects the client's emotional needs

**C.** Consideration of the client's intersectionality with other LGBTQI+ identities

**92.** A social worker is terminating with an older adult client as the social worker will be leaving the agency due to relocation. The client, who has been receiving services for many years from the social worker, gives the social worker some homemade baked goods in appreciation. To handle this situation ethically, the social worker should:

**A.** Accept the gift with an expression of gratitude

**B.** Decline the gift while explaining that gifts cannot be accepted due to ethical standards

**C.** Inform the client that the baked goods will be given to clients in need instead of being used personally

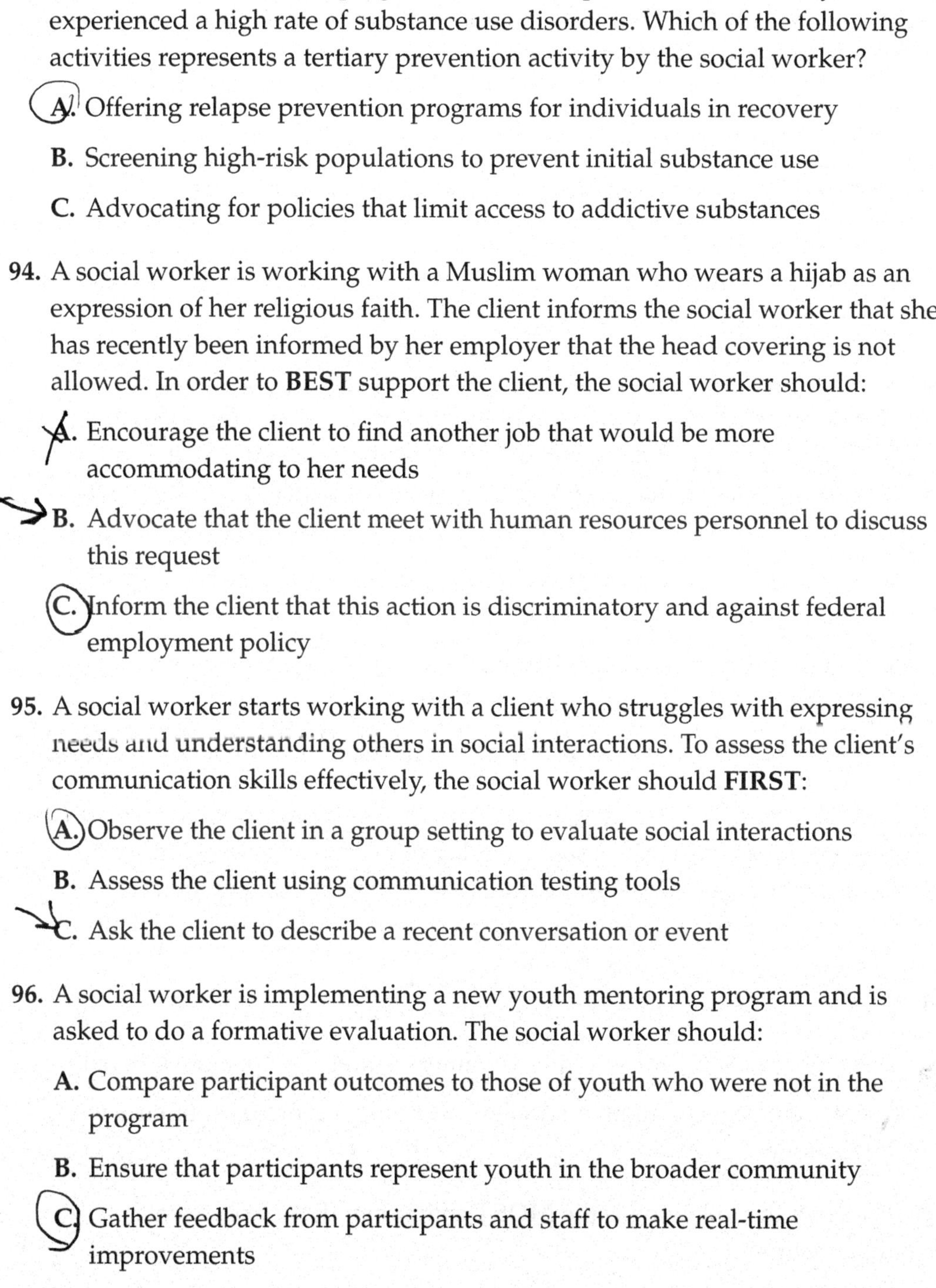

**93.** A social worker is developing an intervention plan for a community that has experienced a high rate of substance use disorders. Which of the following activities represents a tertiary prevention activity by the social worker?

**A.** Offering relapse prevention programs for individuals in recovery

**B.** Screening high-risk populations to prevent initial substance use

**C.** Advocating for policies that limit access to addictive substances

**94.** A social worker is working with a Muslim woman who wears a hijab as an expression of her religious faith. The client informs the social worker that she has recently been informed by her employer that the head covering is not allowed. In order to **BEST** support the client, the social worker should:

**A.** Encourage the client to find another job that would be more accommodating to her needs

**B.** Advocate that the client meet with human resources personnel to discuss this request

**C.** Inform the client that this action is discriminatory and against federal employment policy

**95.** A social worker starts working with a client who struggles with expressing needs and understanding others in social interactions. To assess the client's communication skills effectively, the social worker should **FIRST**:

**A.** Observe the client in a group setting to evaluate social interactions

**B.** Assess the client using communication testing tools

**C.** Ask the client to describe a recent conversation or event

**96.** A social worker is implementing a new youth mentoring program and is asked to do a formative evaluation. The social worker should:

**A.** Compare participant outcomes to those of youth who were not in the program

**B.** Ensure that participants represent youth in the broader community

**C.** Gather feedback from participants and staff to make real-time improvements

**97.** A social worker is working with a client to select the appropriate intervention strategy. Which of the following **BEST** describes the approach that should be taken in this process?

**A.** Relying on the social worker's professional expertise to select the evidence-based practice

**B.** Integrating client preferences and values with the appropriate evidence-based practice

**C.** Asking the client to identify the protocols to maximize empowerment and self-determination

**98.** A social worker is asked by close friends to provide therapy to their adolescent child, who has been struggling with anxiety and depression. The friends insist that the social worker is the best person to help due to their strong relationship. To handle this situation ethically, the social worker should:

**A.** Agree to provide therapy given the importance of the established trust with the family

**B.** Provide the parents with a list of other qualified providers instead of directly providing services

**C.** Ask the parents more about the problems that the youth is experiencing

**99.** A social worker is working with a client who has a problem that is treatment resistant. Evaluation by the social worker indicates no progress made on the target behavior. The social worker has reviewed relevant literature but remains uncertain about next steps. In order to address this situation effectively, the social worker should **NEXT**:

**A.** Seek consultation from professional colleagues

**B.** Ask the client for insight into why interventions do not appear to help

**C.** Refer the client to another social worker who has more experience with this issue

**100.** Which of the following is the **MOST** common indicator of sexual dysfunction?

**A.** Decreased sexual desire

**B.** Difficulty with arousal

**C.** Inability to reach orgasm

**101.** A social worker is treating a client who would like a referral to another social worker specializing in the client's problem. The social worker has treated the problem several times and the social worker's supervisor feels that the social worker is competent to provide needed care. In order to handle the situation appropriately, the social worker should:

**A.** Ask the supervisor to attend the next session to speak with the client about the concerns

**B.** Assure the client that the social worker is able to provide care

**C.** Provide the client with the name and contact information of a referral

**102.** A social worker is part of an interdisciplinary team working with a client who has complex health and social needs. To ensure effective collaboration, the social worker should:

**A.** Help the team to focus on common client goals

**B.** Facilitate group problem-solving and communication

**C.** Respect the professional expertise of each team member

**103.** A social worker is charged with offering an in-service training session in the agency. Which of the following tasks would be **MOST** helpful in designing this offering?

**A.** Reviewing staff job descriptions to identify the skills needed to deliver evidence-based interventions

**B.** Gathering information from professional colleagues about offerings that were valuable to their staff

**C.** Determining licensure requirements for mandatory continuing education topics

**104.** A social worker is providing therapy to a client who is involved in an ongoing legal dispute. The client has shared sensitive information that could potentially be damaging if disclosed in court. The social worker is concerned that the detailed documentation of sessions could be subpoenaed and used against the client in these proceedings. To address this situation ethically, the social worker should:

**A.** Refrain from documenting sensitive information in the client record

**B.** Document using vague language to obscure details that could be harmful

**C.** Ensure that all documentation is objective and relevant to the services provided

**105.** A social worker is facilitating an assertiveness training session for clients who struggle with expressing their needs and setting boundaries. During a session, a client expresses discomfort with the idea of being assertive, stating that it feels too confrontational. The social worker should **NEXT**:

**A.** Encourage the client to practice assertiveness in low-stakes situations

**B.** Explain the difference between assertiveness and aggression to the client

**C.** Explore the client's past experiences with assertiveness

**106.** Which of the following is not required of social workers as part of culturally competent practice?

**A.** Understanding personal biases and engaging in self-correction

**B.** Recognizing clients as experts in their own culture

**C.** Holding clients accountable for advancing cultural humility

**107.** A social worker is preparing a case presentation for a multidisciplinary team which is charged with assisting the social worker in identifying the best course of action for a client. Which of the following is **MOST** helpful to include in the presentation?

**A.** Detailed account of the client's entire history, including childhood experiences

**B.** Summary of the client's current treatment plan and progress toward goals

**C.** Potential interventions that the social worker is considering implementing

**108.** A social worker is instructed by the clinical director in the agency to keep separate psychotherapy notes that are distinct from the client's general medical records. The **MOST** likely reason for the request is to:

**A.** Ensure that the notes are not easily accessible for review by others in the agency

**B.** Allow for more detailed documentation of the therapeutic process

**C.** Protect the client's confidentiality when information is released or court ordered

**109.** A social worker is writing a session note after a meeting with a client who has recently started a new treatment plan. The social worker wants to ensure that the session note accurately reflects the client's progress. Which of the following documents would be **BEST** for the social worker to consult?

**A.** Intake assessment

**B.** Recent treatment plan

**C.** Prior session notes

**110.** A social worker at an agency has advocated for additional services for a client, but the agency's policy strictly limits service provision and has denied the request for an exception. In this situation, the social worker should:

**A.** Adhere to the agency's policy and conclude services

**B.** Seek external funding to provide additional services beyond the agency's limit

**C.** Continue to provide services beyond the policy limit without informing the agency

**111.** Which of the following **BEST** describes the basic tenet of critical race theory (CRT)?

**A.** Racism is inherent in every individual.

**B.** Racism is embedded in structures and woven into public policy.

**C.** Racism is the result of individual biases and prejudices.

**112.** A social worker is meeting with a family who is struggling with the mother's recent diagnosis of Alzheimer's disease. The family wants to support their loved one at home as the disease progresses. In this situation, the social worker should **FIRST**:

**A.** Provide education about the progression of Alzheimer's disease

**B.** Offer counseling to address the family's emotional reactions to the diagnosis

**C.** Connect the family with a local Alzheimer's support group

**113.** A social worker is temporarily covering for a colleague who is out on medical leave due to surgery. To effectively manage client situations, which of the following client documents should the social worker review?

**A.** Intake assessments

**B.** Recent treatment notes

**C.** Current treatment plans

114. A social worker is working with an older adult woman who is being considered for nursing home care. Which of the following should be the focus of the evaluation to determine her appropriateness for such a setting?

A. Instrumental activities of daily living (IADLs)

B. Chronic medical conditions requiring care

C. Activities of daily living (ADLs)

115. A social worker is working with a client who has recently started experiencing memory lapses, difficulty with coordination, and sudden mood swings. The client denies any history of mental health issues but shows no concern about these recent changes. To assist the client, the social worker should **FIRST**:

A. Suggest that the client participate in cognitive behavioral therapy to address the behavioral symptoms

B. Explore the client's recent stressors to understand the cause of any underlying problems

C. Refer the client for a neurological evaluation to assess for possible underlying conditions

116. A social worker is working with a client who has recently been experiencing persistent anxiety and emotional distress. The client reports seeking guidance from a local shaman to assist with coping. In order to **BEST** support the client, the social worker should:

A. Determine the current source of the anxiety and emotional distress

B. Ask the client about how cultural and spiritual practices impact overall well-being

C. Provide therapy in conjunction with recommending continued sessions with the shaman

117. A social worker is charged with establishing a service network for those who have been unable to maintain permanent housing. The social worker crafts an affiliation agreement between two of the largest service providers. The social worker is **MOST** likely engaging in this task to:

A. Establish the services to be provided by each organization

B. Improve coordination of services to avoid duplication

C. Ensure that there is shared responsibility for serving the population

**118.** A social worker at a busy urban agency is feeling increasingly overwhelmed. The workload is exceptionally high, with many clients requiring intensive support. Despite best efforts, the social worker finds it difficult to balance work demands with personal self-care and is beginning to notice a decline in personal mental and physical health. The agency has strict policies regarding workload standards and requires social workers to adhere to set hours and documentation standards. The social worker feels that the lack of adequate self-care is impacting the ability to provide high-quality care to clients and is worried about the potential consequences for well-being and professional effectiveness. In this situation, the social worker should:

**A.** Seek supervision to discuss the impact of the burnout

**B.** Advocate for workplace self-care programs for staff

**C.** Request to reduce the social worker's responsibilities to assist with burnout

**119.** A social worker is working with a client who has recently immigrated from another country to escape a financial crisis due to political conflict in the client's country of origin. To **BEST** support the client's acculturation process, the social worker should:

**A.** Help the client engage in community activities and connect with local support networks

**B.** Work with the client to maintain cultural practices within new social structures and norms

**C.** Assist the client to understand the social structures currently present in the new country

**120.** A hospital social worker is conducting an assessment with a client who has recently started dialysis. The social worker focuses solely on gathering subjective data during the assessment. Which of the following is **MOST** likely the social worker's reason for using this approach?

**A.** The client needs the opportunity to process the experience and its impact on the client's quality of life.

**B.** There is concern that the client may not understand the lifestyle changes needed while receiving dialysis.

**C.** The social worker wants to understand the client's feelings about this recent change in health status.

**121.** Which of the following is an example of social stratification?

**A.** Natural tendency of those with the same economic status to socialize with one another

**B.** Receipt of more opportunities by those who have relatives with higher social status

**C.** Segregation of poor individuals into low-income areas within communities

**122.** In social service organizations, who are the individuals primarily responsible for formally setting the strategic direction?

**A.** Executive directors

**B.** Agency administrators

**C.** Boards of directors

**123.** A social work manager is concerned about the inability of a service organization to consistently meet its goals. The staff report a lack of resources to get their jobs done effectively. In order to **BEST** address this problem, the social worker should:

**A.** Implement a performance-based funding system

**B.** Determine what resources are needed by staff on a daily basis

**C.** Engage in fundraising efforts that would be directed toward meeting staff's unmet needs

**124.** A social worker is employed at a community agency that provides support services for survivors of incest. The current agency policy requires clients to provide detailed personal histories during the initial intake process, which has been reported to be distressing for some clients. To adhere to trauma-informed care principles, the social worker should:

**A.** Advocate that clients are not required to disclose traumatic experiences during intake

**B.** Implement training for staff on how to sensitively collect personal information

**C.** Gather clients' opinions on agency policies to ensure satisfaction

**125.** A social worker in private practice is evaluating the effectiveness of a new cognitive behavioral therapy (CBT) program for clients with anxiety disorders. The study involves randomly assigning clients into two groups. One group receives the new CBT program, while the other group receives the standard treatment. Both groups are assessed before and after the treatment to measure changes in anxiety levels. Which type of research design is the social worker using in this study?

**A.** Quasi-experimental design

**B.** Experimental design

**C.** Preexperimental design

**126.** A social work supervisor is identifying the learning needs of supervisees to develop learning objectives. To **MOST** effectively complete this process, the social worker should:

**A.** Conduct a structured assessment of the supervisees' skills and knowledge gaps

**B.** Observe supervisees during their work to assess their current competencies

**C.** Ask supervisees about their career goals and interests

**127.** A social worker is hired to evaluate the overall functioning of a community organization. The social worker is specifically interested in learning about communication patterns within the organization. Which of the following methods would be **MOST** helpful in collecting relevant data?

**A.** Conducting a survey to gather feedback from staff members on their experiences with internal communication

**B.** Reviewing organizational documents to analyze communication policies and procedures

**C.** Reading agency newsletters and internal memos to identify transparency and tone

**128.** A social worker in an large social service agency is tasked with determining if there are any disparities in dropout rates based on demographic factors. The social worker has access to a large data set that includes comprehensive data with client demographics, service usage history, and outcomes. Which of the following data analysis methods would be **MOST** appropriate for the social worker to use in this situation?

**A.** Descriptive statistics

**B.** Regression analysis

**C.** Content analysis

**129.** A social work administrator is considering replicating a program as there is a significant demand for services. Which of the following program evaluations will be **MOST** helpful in making this decision?

**A.** Summative evaluation

**B.** Formative evaluation

**C.** Cost-benefit evaluation

**130.** A school social worker is evaluating a new intervention program for at-risk youth. The social worker wants to ensure that the measurement tools used are reliable, so the social worker administers them twice to the same pilot group of youth to compare the results. Which of the following methods is the social worker using to assess reliability?

**A.** Test–retest

**B.** Inter-rater

**C.** Internal consistency

**131.** A social worker employed in a juvenile justice facility discovers that a risk assessment used with clients does not contain some important factors that have been determined to indicate clients are at risk for reoffending. Which of the following types of validity is **MOST** at risk based on this discovery?

**A.** Content validity

**B.** Criterion-related validity

**C.** Construct validity

**132.** Which of the following **BEST** describes the latency stage of psychosexual development according to Freud?

**A.** Movement away from sexual desires toward emotional relationships with others

**B.** Development of social skills and focus on academic and extracurricular activities

**C.** Exploration of sexual identity formation based on early psychological desires

**133.** A social work manager is leading a team that is struggling with low morale and inconsistent performance. In order to **MOST** effectively to improve team cohesion, the social worker should:

**A.** Ask team members to engage in cooperative performance monitoring

**B.** Encourage collaborative decision-making

**C.** Delegate tasks to team members based on their strengths

**134.** A social worker is working with a client who consistently downplays substance use, despite evidence of its negative impact on the client's life. The social worker directly confronts the client about the substance usage. The social worker is **MOST** likely using this technique to:

**A.** Help the client to see that the usage is a problem

**B.** Demonstrate that the social worker does not condone the denial

**C.** Direct the conversation to the substance use for further exploration

**135.** When obtaining informed consent from clients, which of the following is the **MOST** important for social workers to ensure?

**A.** Clients understand all risks and benefits of proposed interventions.

**B.** Consent forms are signed by clients and stored in the clients' file.

**C.** Social workers provide all necessary information in a way that clients can easily understand.

136. A social worker is meeting with a client who has been feeling overwhelmed and tearful due to ongoing work-related stress. During the session, the social worker reflects on the client's maladaptive feelings. According to the problem-solving process, which of the following should the social worker say **NEXT**?

- **A.** "It is completely understandable to feel this way given the pressure you have been under."
- **B.** "Please share what you think might be triggering these intense feelings at work."
- **C.** "Let's review what we have talked about and consider your next steps."

137. Which of the following actions is the **MOST** appropriate use of client records?

- **A.** Sharing client records with colleagues during a team meeting to seek advice on treatment options
- **B.** Reviewing the records to refresh the social worker's memory of the client's history and progress
- **C.** Using client records for training purposes to help educate others in the agency about best practices

138. A social worker is employing Bowenian therapy with a family to address ongoing relational issues. The **PRIMARY** aim of this therapeutic approach is to:

- **A.** Increase the emotional closeness and interdependence between family members
- **B.** Improve communication patterns to reduce misunderstandings and conflicts
- **C.** Differentiate the self by helping individuals establish healthier boundaries

139. A social worker is participating in a quality assurance initiative at an agency which aims to improve service delivery and client outcomes. As part of this initiative, the social worker should:

- **A.** Review case records to ensure that documentation meets agency and regulatory standards
- **B.** Increase client engagement by asking clients about enhanced supports needed
- **C.** Advocate for additional staff training on best practice interventions

**140.** A client who has experienced a serious accident is being evaluated for appropriateness for a rehabilitation center or returning directly home. The social worker is part of an interdisciplinary team focused on this determination. Which of the following would **MOST** likely be the deciding factor for determining the client's readiness to return home?

**A.** Ability to perform daily activities

**B.** Client's expressed desire to return home

**C.** Long-term prognosis for independence

**141.** A social worker is meeting with a client who is feeling anxious and overwhelmed due to recent changes in the client's job role. The client is unsure about how to handle these changes. Which of the following statements by the social worker would be **BEST** in this situation?

**A.** "It sounds like you're feeling overwhelmed. Let's talk about some ways to manage your anxiety and stress."

**B.** "Many people face similar challenges. It is important to stay positive and keep pushing forward."

**C.** "Could you describe more about the specific changes in your job role that are making you feel unsupported?"

**142.** A social worker discovers that a client falsified information on the application for a public assistance program, which the social worker completed on the client's behalf. The client insists on continuing to provide this false information to secure the benefits. In this situation, the social worker should:

**A.** Support the client by providing false information to ensure the client receives the benefits

**B.** Report the issue to the appropriate authorities after discussing the situation with the client

**C.** Advise the client of the risks associated with continuing to provide false information

**143.** A school social worker is charged with developing a behavioral plan for an 8-year-old student who has difficulty using the bathroom independently. The social worker works with the student on tasks associated with bathroom usage such as locking the door, washing hands, locating the bathroom, and using toilet paper. Once the student has demonstrated the ability to do each task independently, the social worker helps sequence them into mastery of the entire routine. Which of the following techniques is the social worker **MOST** likely using?

**A.** Chaining

**B.** Shaping

**C.** Modeling

**144.** Which of the following describes ego-dystonic behavior by a client?

**A.** Being distressed by compulsive handwashing despite knowing it is excessive

**B.** Consistently arriving late for important meetings late

**C.** Suffering from depressive episodes that threaten self-worth and well-being

**145.** A social worker is working with a client who has been resistant to making recommended lifestyle changes related to health problems. To **MOST** effectively assess the client's motivation to change, the social worker should:

**A.** Explore the client's understanding of the consequences of the current behavior

**B.** Assess whether the client has taken any actions to modify negative behaviors

**C.** Determine if the client believes in the client's personal ability to make sustained change

**146.** Which of the following **BEST** describes the role of a social worker in helping a client with a chronic mental illness?

**A.** Providing clinical counseling and medication management focused on the illness

**B.** Coordinating services and support to help the client manage the illness

**C.** Promoting independence and role fulfillment that may be compromised by the illness

**147.** A social worker is conducting a mental status examination with a client who has presented with significant mood changes and confusion. The social worker is **MOST** likely performing this assessment to:

**A.** Determine the client's ability to engage in ongoing therapy

**B.** Evaluate the client's current safety

**C.** Assess the client's current functioning

**148.** A social worker in a mental health agency is asked by a supervisor to identify whether a client should be evaluated for an involuntary commitment. Which of the following factors would be **MOST** helpful in making the decision?

**A.** Inability to make progress in long-term treatment

**B.** Prior incidents of self-harm or violence

**C.** Current assaultive behavior

**149.** A school social worker is preparing to gather sensitive information from a student regarding past trauma. Which of the following data collection methods is **MOST** effective in soliciting this information?

**A.** Structured interview

**B.** Open-ended assessment

**C.** Written survey or questionnaire

**150.** A social worker is assisting a client who is seeking ongoing substance abuse treatment and is facing challenges in maintaining sobriety, managing stress, and accessing support services. The client has received detoxification services but needs to sustain recovery. The social worker should **FIRST:**

**A.** Learn more about the client's triggers and history of use

**B.** Develop a relapse prevention plan with the client

**C.** Connect the client with local support groups and resources for ongoing recovery support

151. A social worker is working with a community that is experiencing challenges related to economic development and social cohesion. There is widespread disagreement about the nature of the problems. In order to facilitate social change, the social worker should:

   A. Identify the power structures in place that need to be leveraged for community development

   B. Ask community leaders to assist with helping define the most pressing issues

   C. Facilitate a community discussion to develop a common identification of the concerns

152. A social worker is beginning to work with a client who the social worker believes has suffered significant trauma in the past. To determine whether trauma has been experienced, the social worker should **FIRST**:

   A. Use a standardized trauma assessment tool to screen the client for trauma

   B. Explore the client's current coping mechanisms and emotional responses to triggers

   C. Conduct a biopsychosocial assessment to understand the client's overall life context

153. A social worker is assessing a client who struggles with issues related to self-image. When doing an assessment of the client, which of the following factors needs to be the focus of the social worker's inquiry?

   A. Negative feedback and criticism from significant others

   B. Personal history of achievement and success

   C. Awareness of societal trends and media portrayals of beauty

154. A school social worker is working with a student who has been struggling academically and has shown signs of frustration and low self-esteem in the classroom. The social worker decides to incorporate an educational test into the assessment process. The social worker is **MOST** likely using the educational test to:

   A. Identify the student's specific learning strengths and weaknesses

   B. Compare the student's performance with that of the student's peers

   C. Diagnose the student with a learning disability

**155.** A social worker is meeting with a client who has recently been referred for a substance abuse evaluation. The client mentions having trouble at work and feeling increasingly isolated from friends and family. Additionally, the social worker notices that the client appears disheveled and has bloodshot eyes with dilated pupils. Which of the following signs is **MOST** indicative of drug misuse?

**A.** Trouble at work and increased isolation from friends and family

**B.** Appearing disheveled and having bloodshot eyes with dilated pupils

**C.** Changes in sleep patterns and appetite

**156.** A social worker gets a referral for a new client who has difficulty making decisions without excessive reassurance from others and fears not being able to perform routine tasks independently. The client often goes to great lengths to avoid being abandoned, even if it means tolerating mistreatment. Which of the following diagnoses **BEST** fits these characteristics?

**A.** Borderline personality disorder

**B.** Avoidant personality disorder

**C.** Dependent personality disorder

**157.** A social worker is meeting with a client who has been experiencing persistent symptoms of depression, including low energy, loss of interest in activities, and changes in sleep patterns. The client mentions that they have been prescribed medication to help manage these symptoms which resulted in the doctor advising the client to avoid certain foods, such as aged cheeses and cured meats. Which of the following types of antidepressants is the client **MOST** likely taking?

**A.** Selective serotonin reuptake inhibitor (SSRI)

**B.** Monoamine oxidase inhibitor (MAOI)

**C.** Tricyclic antidepressant (TCA)

**158.** A social worker is treating a client who has been experiencing depression and is considering terminating therapy sessions due to financial difficulties. The social worker knows of a scholarship fund within the agency that could cover the client's remaining sessions but is not supposed to disclose this information. The social worker should:

**A.** Disclose the scholarship fund to the client even though it is against agency policy

**B.** Assist the client to find other ways to treat the depression

**C.** Discuss the client's financial difficulties with a supervisor to explore potential options

**159.** A social worker is assessing a client with various behavioral issues. The social worker decides to use multiple sources of information, including clinical interviews, client self-reports, and input from family members, to achieve a more accurate and reliable understanding of the client's issues. Which of the following methods describes the social worker's approach?

**A.** Systematic review

**B.** Data triangulation

**C.** Needs assessment

**160.** The reason that public defender offices for those arrested for crimes have expanded their practices to include social workers is to:

**A.** Provide legal advice on immigration status and housing issues

**B.** Reduce the negative effects of unsupported reentry leading to recidivism

**C.** Engage in litigation related to government assistance programs

**161.** Which of the following is the **BEST** definition of a carceral system?

**A.** Policies and institutions that define criminal activity and punish those engaging in such activity

**B.** Programs aimed at reducing crime rates through all types of preventive measures

**C.** System of support services for perpetrators and victims affected by crime

**162.** Upon intake, a social worker learns that a client has a complex family background with many separations, deaths, and intergenerational trauma. The social worker asks the client to create a visual representation of the client's family relationships, including connections and patterns across generations. Which of the following assessment tools is the social worker utilizing with this client?

**A.** Genogram

**B.** Ecomap

**C.** Client self-report

**163.** A social worker is approached by a former client who asks to connect on social media. The former client states that they would like to keep in touch with the social worker. In this situation, the social worker should:

**A.** Accept the request to maintain a supportive connection with the former client

**B.** Decline the request to maintain professional boundaries

**C.** Ignore the request to avoid any potential ethical dilemmas

**164.** A social worker is working with a family that has recently experienced a significant crisis. Members of the family have faced a sudden job loss, a major health issue, and the death of a close relative. The family members are struggling to cope with these changes. In order to **BEST** assist this family, the social worker should:

**A.** Build resilience to strengthen the family's ability to handle future stressors and crises

**B.** Restore the family's daily routines and emotional state to before crisis levels

**C.** Explore the impact of these events on communication and relationship patterns

**165.** When doing an assessment with a client, a social worker decides to use an ecomap. The social worker is **MOST** likely using this tool to:

**A.** Assess family history and generational patterns

**B.** Identify support systems and interactions with community resources

**C.** Evaluate emotional responses and resilience to past traumas

**166.** A social worker is evaluating a client who has recently been experiencing a sense of spiritual disconnection given significant disruptions in daily life. The client reports a history of chronic health issues, recent job loss, and strained relationships with family members. During the assessment phase, the social worker should **FIRST**:

**A.** Address the client's biological health issues

**B.** Explore the client's spiritual disconnection

**C.** Understand any connection between these problems

**167.** A social worker is working with a family in which the 12-year-old child has taken on many responsibilities typically handled by parents, such as caring for younger siblings and managing household tasks. The parents rely heavily on the child for emotional support, often confiding in the child about financial and marital issues. Which of the following is **MOST** likely a consequence for the child of this role reversal?

**A.** Resilience in adulthood

**B.** Difficulty in forming peer relationships

**C.** Poor self-image

**168.** A social worker is gathering information from a client to better understand mental health and daily functioning. Which of the following self-reporting methods should be considered?

**A.** Journaling

**B.** Behavioral tracking

**C.** Observation

**169.** A social worker is assessing a child who has experienced significant traumatic events. The child shows signs of severe emotional difficulties, including an inability to form secure attachments and engaging in overly familiar behavior with strangers. Which of the following diagnoses **BEST** fits these symptoms?

**A.** Reactive attachment disorder (RAD)

**B.** Disinhibited social engagement disorder (DSED)

**C.** Posttraumatic stress disorder (PTSD)

**170.** A school social worker is asked to observe a child in a classroom to provide an opinion of the child's readiness for more mainstream activities. The child has worked with the social worker in the past and is excited about the classroom visit. Which of the following is **MOST** likely a concern about this approach?

**A.** The recommendation may negatively impact the existing relationship with the child.

**B.** The child may act differently during the class session due to the knowledge of being observed.

**C.** The social worker should not provide an opinion without discussions with other professionals.

# Answers With Analytic Rationales

1. **Correct Answer:** C. OCD is distressing for the individual with the condition, whereas OCPD is problematic for others.

   **Rationale:** OCD is characterized by intrusive, distressing thoughts (obsessions) and repetitive behaviors or mental acts (compulsions) that individuals feel compelled to perform. These symptoms are highly distressing to the person with OCD, causing significant anxiety and often interfering with daily functioning. Individuals with OCD are usually aware that their obsessions and compulsions are irrational but feel unable to control them. OCPD, on the other hand, is a personality disorder marked by a chronic preoccupation with orderliness, perfectionism, and control. People with OCPD tend to have a rigid and inflexible approach to life, often imposing their standards and expectations on others. Unlike OCD, individuals with OCPD usually do not find their behavior distressing; instead, they often see their need for order and control as rational and appropriate. However, their behavior can be problematic for others around them, especially in personal and professional relationships, where their inflexibility can lead to conflict. The response choice that states that OCD focuses on order and control while OCPD involves obsessions and compulsions reverses the characteristics of the two disorders. OCD involves obsessions and compulsions, while OCPD is characterized by a focus on order, control, and perfectionism. Both disorders can be addressed with therapy, but the nature of the distress caused by each BEST defines the difference.

   **Question Type:** Recall

**Content Area:** Assessment, Diagnosis, and Treatment Planning (The use of the Diagnostic and Statistical Manual of the American Psychiatric Association)

2. **Correct Answer:** A. Encourage the client to participate in social activities offered by the facility

   **Rationale:** Encouraging the client to engage in social activities within the assisted living facility is the most effective way to help them build new relationships and reduce feelings of loneliness. Social interactions can significantly enhance the client's sense of belonging and ease adjustment to the new environment. While helping the client accept the loss of the spouse and arranging visits with others are important, participating in social activities directly addresses the client's current struggle with loneliness and promotes a more active and fulfilling daily life in the new surroundings, which was mentioned in the question. The client's issues are not directly related to the loss of the spouse so dealing with the loss is not the primary problem.

   **Question Type:** Reasoning

   **Content Area:** Human Development, Diversity, and Behavior in the Environment (Gerontology)

3. **Correct Answer:** C. Attempt to manage intense emotional pain and distress

   **Rationale:** Self-cutting behavior is MOST commonly associated with an attempt to manage intense emotional pain and distress. It serves as a coping mechanism to provide temporary relief from overwhelming emotions. While feeling disconnected from social relationships can contribute to emotional distress, it is not the primary cause of self-cutting behavior. Self-cutting is more directly related to managing intense emotional pain and distress. The behavior serves as a coping mechanism for overwhelming feelings, providing temporary relief from emotional suffering. Disconnection from social relationships might be a contributing factor to the distress, but the act of self-cutting is primarily aimed at addressing the internal emotional pain rather than the external social disconnection.

   **Question Type:** Recall

   **Content Area:** Assessment, Diagnosis, and Treatment Planning (Methods to assess the client's/client system's coping abilities)

4. **Correct Answer:** B. Engage in conjoint sessions to work on communication and conflict resolution

   **Rationale:** Conjoint sessions involve both the woman and her teenage child meeting with the social worker together to address their relationship issues directly. This approach BEST allows the social worker to observe their interactions, facilitate communication, and work on resolving conflicts in a structured setting. It is especially effective in addressing the emotional distancing and arguments that are affecting their relationship, as it provides a space for them to collaborate on improving their communication and understanding each other's perspectives. Providing suggestions during individual therapy may not fully address the dynamic between the woman and her child, as it does not involve direct interaction between them in a therapeutic setting. Referring them to a support group can be helpful but is less focused on their specific relationship issues and may not address their communication difficulties as effectively as conjoint sessions. Additionally, the question asks for the answer which represents the social worker assisting; when these clients are joining a support group, the group is the agent of change.

**Question Type:** Reasoning

**Content Area:** Psychotherapy, Clinical Interventions, and Case Management (Family therapy models, interventions, and approaches)

5. **Correct Answer:** C. Helping the client recognize and label personal emotions properly

   **Rationale:** Dialectical behavior therapy (DBT) begins by focusing on fundamental skills that help clients with BPD manage their intense emotions. The FIRST step in DBT is often to help clients recognize and accurately label their emotions. This is crucial because many individuals with BPD experience emotional dysregulation, where their emotions can be overwhelming and difficult to identify or understand. By learning to recognize and label their emotions, clients can gain better control over their emotional responses and work toward more effective regulation strategies. While rebuilding relationships and establishing support systems is important, DBT typically starts with individual skills training before addressing broader relational issues. Building relationships often comes later in the therapy process, once clients have developed a foundation of emotional regulation and interpersonal effectiveness skills. Addressing practical issues like employment and financial stability is important but is generally not the initial focus of DBT. The therapy first aims to stabilize the client's emotional state to better handle life's challenges, including financial issues, once emotional regulation skills are in place.

   **Question Type:** Application

   **Content Area:** Psychotherapy, Clinical Interventions, and Case Management (Cognitive and behavioral interventions)

6. **Correct Answer:** C. Cyclothymic disorder

   **Rationale:** The child's symptoms, which include mood swings with hypomanic and depressive episodes over the past year, MOST closely align with cyclothymic disorder. Cyclothymic disorder is characterized by numerous periods of hypomanic symptoms and depressive symptoms that do not meet the criteria for a full manic or major depressive episode. This disorder requires symptoms to be present for at least 1 year in children and adolescents, which matches the child's reported duration. Bipolar I disorder involves experiencing at least one full manic episode, which lasts for at least a week (or any duration if hospitalization is required), and often includes periods of major depressive episodes. The child's description does not indicate the presence of a full manic episode, so bipolar I disorder is not the most accurate diagnosis. Bipolar II disorder is defined by having at least one hypomanic episode (lasting at least 4 days) and one major depressive episode. The child's symptoms, while involving periods of elevated mood and depressive symptoms, do not reach the severity of a full major depressive episode or a hypomanic episode as required for bipolar II disorder.

   **Question Type:** Application

   **Content Area:** Assessment, Diagnosis, and Treatment Planning (The use of the Diagnostic and Statistical Manual of the American Psychiatric Association)

7. **Correct Answer:** A. Malingering

   **Rationale:** Malingering refers to the intentional production or exaggeration of physical or psychological symptoms for external gain, such as financial compensation or avoiding responsibilities. In this scenario, the client is primarily concerned with obtaining financial compensation and avoiding responsibilities, which BEST aligns with the concept of malingering. Somatization involves experiencing and reporting physical symptoms without intentional deceit. The symptoms are genuine from the perspective of the individual but are not intentionally produced for external benefits. Since the client's primary goal is financial compensation and not an expression of genuine distress, this does not fit somatization. Sublimation is a defense mechanism where an individual channels unacceptable impulses into socially acceptable activities. It is not relevant to the client's condition described here, as the focus is on external gain rather than a psychological defense mechanism.

   **Question Type:** Application

   **Content Area:** Assessment, Diagnosis, and Treatment Planning (The indicators of feigning illness)

8. **Correct Answer:** A. Discuss the issues that have prevented treatment in the past

   **Rationale:** Given the client's ambivalence about seeking additional support and reluctance to engage in therapy, the most appropriate FIRST step is to explore the issues that have hindered treatment in the past. Understanding these barriers can provide insight into the client's resistance and help tailor a more effective approach to address specific concerns. This approach allows the social worker to address underlying issues, build rapport, and create a more supportive environment for the client to reengage in therapy. Identifying small steps and determining the root cause are also important but are often more effective once the barriers to treatment are clearly understood and addressed.

   **Question Type:** Reasoning

   **Content Area:** Psychotherapy, Clinical Interventions, and Case Management (Problem-solving models and approaches [e.g., brief, solution-focused methods or techniques])

9. **Correct Answer:** A. Disruptive mood dysregulation disorder (DMDD)

   **Rationale:** DMDD is characterized by severe, recurrent temper outbursts that are out of proportion to the situation and inconsistent with the child's developmental level. These outbursts occur frequently (on average, three or more times per week), and the child exhibits a persistently irritable or angry mood between outbursts. The symptoms must be present for at least 12 months and must occur in multiple settings (e.g., at home, school, with peers). Given that the child in the scenario has been experiencing intense, frequent outbursts and a persistently irritable mood for over a year, DMDD is the MOST likely diagnosis. While conduct disorder involves a pattern of behavior that violates the rights of others or societal norms, it typically includes more severe behaviors such as aggression toward people or animals, destruction of property, deceitfulness, or theft. The scenario describes outbursts and irritability, but it does not mention the persistent, severe rule-breaking behaviors characteristic of conduct disorder. ODD is characterized by a pattern of angry/irritable mood, argumentative/defiant behavior, or vindictiveness. However, the level of irritability and frequency of temper outbursts described in the scenario is more intense than typically seen in ODD and better aligns with DMDD. The persistently irritable mood between outbursts is a key differentiating factor that points to DMDD rather than ODD.

   **Question Type:** Application

   **Content Area:** Assessment, Diagnosis, and Treatment Planning (The use of the Diagnostic and Statistical Manual of the American Psychiatric Association)

10. **Correct Answer:** B. Sertraline (Zoloft)

**Rationale:** Sertraline (Zoloft) is a selective serotonin reuptake inhibitor (SSRI) MOST commonly prescribed to treat MDD. It helps alleviate symptoms of depression such as persistent sadness, loss of interest in daily activities, and difficulty concentrating by increasing levels of serotonin in the brain. Risperidone (Risperdal) is an antipsychotic medication used primarily for schizophrenia, not for MDD. Diazepam (Valium) is an anxiolytic that treats anxiety but is not typically prescribed as a primary treatment for MDD.

**Question Type:** Application

**Content Area:** Assessment, Diagnosis, and Treatment Planning (Common psychotropic and non-psychotropic prescriptions and over-the-counter medications and their side effects)

11. **Correct Answer:** B. Elevated blood marker results

**Rationale:** Elevated blood marker results can be crucial in understanding potential complications or underlying issues related to the chronic health condition. Addressing the implications of these results is MOST important for guiding appropriate medical follow-up and interventions. While the social and emotional effects and the self-care regimen are also important, the elevated blood marker results provide key insights into the client's current health status and necessary medical actions. A physical condition may be responsible for the symptoms, which will mitigate the impact of good self-care. Physical health also needs to take precedent over social and emotional effects given these recent results.

**Question Type:** Reasoning

**Content Area:** Assessment, Diagnosis, and Treatment Planning (The types of information available from other sources [e.g., agency, employment, medical, psychological, legal, or school records])

12. **Correct Answer:** A. Fear of abandonment

**Rationale:** BPD is MOST often characterized by intense and unstable emotions, impulsive behaviors, and difficulties in relationships. A prominent feature of BPD is an intense fear of abandonment, leading individuals to go to great lengths to avoid perceived or real abandonment, whether through clinging behaviors or emotional outbursts. Compulsive adherence to rules is more characteristic of obsessive-compulsive personality disorder (OCPD), in which individuals are preoccupied with orderliness, perfectionism, and control. Grandiosity of self is typically associated with narcissistic personality disorder, in which individuals have an inflated sense of self-importance and a need for admiration. This is not a primary feature of BPD.

**Question Type:** Application

**Content Area:** Assessment, Diagnosis, and Treatment Planning (The use of the Diagnostic and Statistical Manual of the American Psychiatric Association)

13. **Correct Answer:** B. Borderline personality disorder

**Rationale:** The themes of abandonment, rejection, and distrust revealed in the TAT are MOST strongly associated with borderline personality disorder (BPD). Individuals with BPD often experience intense fears of abandonment and may have unstable interpersonal relationships characterized by alternating between extremes of idealization and devaluation. These patterns align with the themes identified in the TAT. While distrust is a feature of paranoid disorders, the themes of abandonment and rejection are less central to paranoia compared to BPD. Paranoia typically involves pervasive suspicion and mistrust rather than fears of abandonment. Avoidant personality disorder involves social inhibition, feelings of inadequacy, and hypersensitivity to negative evaluation, but it is more characterized by avoidance of social situations rather than intense fears of abandonment and rejection.

**Question Type:** Application

**Content Area:** Assessment, Diagnosis, and Treatment Planning (Techniques and instruments used to assess clients/client systems)

14. **Correct Answer:** A. Sympathy and attention

**Rationale:** Both FDIS and FDIA are MOST often associated with a need for sympathy and attention. Individuals with FDIS fabricate or exaggerate their own symptoms to gain emotional support and validation. Similarly, those with FDIA induce or fabricate symptoms in another person to receive attention and sympathy for themselves. In contrast, external rewards or incentives are characteristic of malingering, not factitious disorders. Fear of abandonment may be relevant in various psychological contexts but is not the primary motivator for these disorders, which center around seeking emotional attention rather than tangible rewards or addressing relational fears.

**Question Type:** Recall

**Content Area:** Assessment, Diagnosis, and Treatment Planning (The use of the Diagnostic and Statistical Manual of the American Psychiatric Association)

15. **Correct Answer:** B. Conversion

**Rationale:** The client is MOST likely using conversion as a defense mechanism, which involves unconsciously transforming psychological stress or conflict into physical symptoms. In this scenario, the client's unexplained physical symptoms, such as difficulty walking, have no medical basis but coincide with the acceptance of a stressful new job. This suggests that the client's emotional stress is being expressed through physical ailments, a hallmark of conversion. Repression involves unconsciously pushing distressing thoughts out of awareness, and displacement involves redirecting emotions to a less threatening target, but neither explains the direct manifestation of physical symptoms in response to stress.

**Question Type:** Application

**Content Area:** Human Development, Diversity, and Behavior in the Environment (Psychological defense mechanisms and their effects on behavior and relationships)

16. **Correct Answer:** B. Conversion

    **Rationale:** In this scenario, the client is exhibiting physical symptoms, such as headaches and stomachaches, with no identifiable medical causes. This is MOST likely indicative of conversion, a defense mechanism where psychological distress is manifested as physical symptoms. The client does not acknowledge the stress, but denial does not include experiencing physical symptoms. Projection is also incorrect as the social worker is not attributing feelings to someone else. The client is using conversion to cope with stress. The social worker should focus on exploring the underlying psychological stress contributing to these physical complaints to provide effective support.

    **Question Type:** Application

    **Content Area:** Human Development, Diversity, and Behavior in the Environment (Psychological defense mechanisms and their effects on behavior and relationships)

17. **Correct Answer:** C. Throughout the helping process

    **Rationale:** Social workers should discuss with clients and other interested parties the nature of confidentiality and limitations of clients' rights to confidentiality. Social workers should review (with clients) circumstances where confidential information may be requested and where disclosure of confidential information may be legally required. This discussion BEST occurs as soon as possible in the social worker–client relationship and as needed throughout the course of the relationship. Only the correct answer identifies the ongoing nature of confidentiality discussions.

    **Question Type:** Recall

**Content Area:** Professional Values and Ethics (Legal and/or ethical issues regarding confidentiality, including electronic information security)

18. **Correct Answer:** B. Request that the court withdraw or limit the order

    **Rationale:** Social workers should protect the confidentiality of clients during legal proceedings to the extent permitted by law. When a court of law or other legally authorized body orders social workers to disclose confidential or privileged information without a client's consent and such disclosure could cause harm to the client, social workers should request that the court withdraw the order or limit the order as narrowly as possible or maintain the records under seal, unavailable for public inspection.

    **Question Type:** Reasoning

    **Content Area:** Professional Values and Ethics (Legal and/or ethical issues regarding confidentiality, including electronic information security)

19. **Correct Answer:** B. Add an addendum to the original note that includes an explanation of the error

    **Rationale:** In this situation, the social worker should follow ethical guidelines that emphasize the importance of maintaining accurate and transparent records. The appropriate action is to NEXT add an addendum to the original case note that corrects the error and provides an explanation. This method ensures that the original document remains intact and that any changes are clearly documented, preserving the integrity of the client's record. Replacing the original note could be viewed as altering the record, which is not transparent and could be ethically and legally problematic. While seeking supervision or consultation can be helpful, the social worker's actions should not be driven by the agency policy or the views of the supervisor. The supervisor may not be a social worker and may advise the social worker to act in a manner that is not considered ethical by social work standards.

    **Question Type:** Reasoning

    **Content Area:** Professional Values and Ethics (Legal and/or ethical issues regarding documentation)

20. **Correct Answer:** A. Preference for solitude

    **Rationale:** Schizoid personality disorder is characterized by a pervasive pattern of detachment from social relationships and a restricted range of emotional expression in interpersonal settings. Individuals with this disorder MOST often prefer solitude and tend to avoid close relationships, not because of fear, anxiety, or distrust but because they genuinely prefer to be alone and are indifferent to social interactions. Bizarre and odd behavior is more characteristic of schizotypal personality disorder, where individuals might have eccentric behaviors or thoughts that can make relationships challenging. Pervasive distrust of others is more closely associated with paranoid personality disorder, where individuals avoid relationships due to a deep suspicion and distrust of others. This is not the main issue in schizoid personality disorder, in which the preference for solitude is voluntary and based on a lack of desire for close connections rather than distrust.

**Question Type:** Recall

**Content Area:** Assessment, Diagnosis, and Treatment Planning (The use of the Diagnostic and Statistical Manual of the American Psychiatric Association)

21. **Correct Answer:** A. Risk of developing serious infections

    **Rationale:** Clozaril (clozapine) is known for its effectiveness in treating treatment-resistant schizophrenia, but it also comes with significant risks that require close monitoring. One of the MOST critical side effects associated with Clozaril is agranulocytosis, a severe reduction in white blood cells that increases the risk of serious infections. Therefore, regular blood tests are required to monitor the white blood cell count and ensure it remains within a safe range. While weight gain is a more common issue with Clozaril, weight loss and malnutrition are not typically primary concerns directly related to its use. Monitoring weight changes is important but is secondary to the more immediate risk of agranulocytosis. Excessive salivation is a known side effect of Clozaril, but it is generally less critical compared to the risk of serious infections. Managing excessive salivation is important but does not outweigh the necessity of monitoring for agranulocytosis, which can have life-threatening consequences.

    **Question Type:** Recall

    **Content Area:** Assessment, Diagnosis, and Treatment Planning (Common psychotropic and non-psychotropic prescriptions and over-the-counter medications and their side effects)

22. **Correct Answer:** A. Repression

    **Rationale:** The client's inability to recall details of the traumatic event and the lack of emotional response are key indicators of repression. Repression is a defense mechanism in which distressing thoughts or memories are unconsciously blocked from entering conscious awareness. Although the client also insists that the event was not serious, which could suggest denial, the primary issue here is the difficulty in recalling details of the event, MOST characteristic of repression. Denial involves rejecting the reality or seriousness of the event, which is different from the client's struggle with memory recall and emotional detachment. Reaction formation involves expressing the opposite of what is truly felt, which is not evident in this scenario.

**Question Type:** Application

**Content Area:** Human Development, Diversity, and Behavior in the Environment (Psychological defense mechanisms and their effects on behavior and relationships)

23. **Correct Answer:** A. Summarize progress and future needs with the client

    **Rationale:** Before terminating the therapeutic relationship, it is crucial for the social worker to summarize the client's progress and discuss future needs. This NEXT step ensures that the client acknowledges and reflects on achievements and understands continued needs moving forward. These actions also provide an opportunity to address any final concerns and solidify the client's readiness for termination, making sure they feel confident and prepared to manage anxiety independently. While reviewing coping skills and identifying community-based supports are important, summarizing progress and future needs directly addresses the client's readiness and ensures a comprehensive wrap-up of the therapeutic process.

    **Question Type:** Reasoning

    **Content Area:** Psychotherapy, Clinical Interventions, and Case Management (Problem-solving models and approaches [e.g., brief, solution-focused methods or techniques])

24. **Correct Answer:** C. Self-medication model

    **Rationale:** The self-medication model suggests that individuals use substances as a way to manage or alleviate underlying psychological or emotional issues. This model views addiction as a means of self-treating symptoms, such as anxiety, depression, or trauma, rather than solely as a result of the addictive properties of substances or learned behaviors. The disease model focuses on addiction as a chronic brain disorder, while the family model emphasizes the role of family dynamics and relationships in addiction.

    **Question Type:** Recall

    **Content Area:** Human Development, Diversity, and Behavior in the Environment (Addiction theories and concepts)

25. **Correct Answer:** B. Obtain informed consent from all participants, ensuring they fully understand the purpose of the study, the procedures involved, potential risks, and their right to withdraw at any time

**Rationale:** Obtaining informed consent is the most critical step to ensure ethical research involving human subjects. Informed consent ensures that participants are fully aware of the study's purpose, procedures, potential risks, and the right to withdraw at any time without facing any consequences. This process respects participants' autonomy and ensures they voluntarily agree to participate with a clear understanding of what the study involves. While developing a detailed research proposal and obtaining IRB approval is crucial for ethical and methodological review, it does not directly address participants' rights and understanding. Securing funding and resources is important for the study's feasibility and success, but it does not replace the need for informed consent.

**Question Type:** Recall

**Content Area:** Professional Values and Ethics (Research ethics [e.g., institutional review boards, use of human subjects, informed consent])

26. **Correct Answer:** A. Establish a contract with the client for the next phase of treatment

**Rationale:** In preparing a client for a transition from intensive therapy to a maintenance phase, it is crucial to NEXT establish a clear contract (i.e., service plan) that outlines goals, responsibilities, and follow-up plans. This contract serves as a formal agreement that details how the client will continue to work on goals, manage challenges, and utilize resources during the maintenance phase. While discussing the client's feelings about the reduction in service levels and monitoring progress are important aspects of the process, the contract provides a structured approach to ensure that both the client and the social worker are aligned on expectations and responsibilities moving forward. This helps to maintain accountability and support the client's continued progress.

**Question Type:** Reasoning

**Content Area:** Psychotherapy, Clinical Interventions, and Case Management (Problem-solving models and approaches [e.g., brief, solution-focused methods or techniques])

27. **Correct Answer:** B. Need to ensure that sharing the experience will not distract the client from addressing personal needs

**Rationale:** When deciding whether to self-disclose personal experiences, the MOST important consideration is to ensure that the disclosure does not distract from the clients' focus on their own needs and challenges. Social workers' primary responsibility is to support clients' therapeutic process by addressing their specific issues and emotional needs. Any self-disclosure should enhance clients' understanding and coping without shifting the focus away from clients' situations or creating a new focus on the social workers' experiences. Building rapport can be beneficial, but it should not take precedence over maintaining clients' focus on their own issues. Providing solutions based on personal experience can be risky, as it may not be applicable to clients' unique situations and can detract from a client-centered approach that emphasizes clients' own solutions and coping strategies.

**Question Type:** Application

**Content Area:** Professional Values and Ethics (Self-disclosure principles and applications)

28. **Correct Answer:** A. Discuss what the client can expect as part of the helping process

    **Rationale:** When beginning work with a new client, especially one who is hesitant and has concerns, it is crucial to FIRST address and alleviate these concerns. By discussing what the client can expect from the therapeutic process, the social worker helps to build trust and establish a foundation for engagement. This step involves explaining the nature of therapy, confidentiality, and the goals of treatment, which can help in reducing anxiety and increasing the client's comfort and willingness to participate. While outlining potential goals and asking about the client's motivation are important tasks, addressing the client's immediate concerns about the process is essential for effective engagement.

    **Question Type:** Reasoning

    **Content Area:** Psychotherapy, Clinical Interventions, and Case Management (Problem-solving models and approaches [e.g., brief, solution-focused methods or techniques])

29. **Correct Answer:** B. Explore the client's reasoning for the decision

    **Rationale:** The NEXT step for the social worker is to explore the client's reasoning behind the decision. This approach ensures that the social worker understands the client's perspective and the factors influencing the choice. By discussing the client's rationale, the social worker can provide targeted support and guidance, helping the client reflect on potential consequences and consider alternative options. Educating the client that the decision is not advised could be perceived as directive and may not fully address the client's individual reasoning or engage the client in a collaborative process. Helping the client identify alternative courses of action is valuable but may be more effective after understanding the client's reasoning and concerns, allowing for a more tailored and supportive discussion of alternatives.

**Question Type:** Reasoning

**Content Area:** Professional Values and Ethics (Techniques for protecting and enhancing client/client system self-determination)

30. **Correct Answer:** A. Clarify the session start and end times and emphasize the importance of punctuality

    **Rationale:** The social worker's primary responsibility in this scenario is to establish clear boundaries and set expectations with the client. By clarifying the session start and end times and emphasizing the importance of punctuality, the social worker addresses the root of the problem directly and helps the client understand the impact of the behavior on the therapeutic process. This approach fosters respect for the therapeutic relationship and encourages the client to take responsibility for participation in the sessions. The incorrect response choices focus on accommodating the client's behavior without addressing the underlying issue, which may reinforce the problematic behavior rather than correcting it.

    **Question Type:** Reasoning

    **Content Area:** Psychotherapy, Clinical Interventions, and Case Management (Limit-setting techniques)

31. **Correct Answer:** B. Role model appropriate boundary-setting behaviors during client interactions

    **Rationale:** Role modeling is an effective technique for supervisors to demonstrate the behaviors they want to instill in their supervisees. By role modeling appropriate boundary setting during client interactions, the supervisor provides the supervisee with a live example of how to manage emotionally charged situations while maintaining professional boundaries. This method not only illustrates the desired behavior but also allows the supervisee to observe and learn in a real-world context. While conducting a training session or assigning readings can be helpful, these approaches are more theoretical and may not have the immediate impact or practical application that role modeling provides.

    **Question Type:** Reasoning

    **Content Area:** Psychotherapy, Clinical Interventions, and Case Management (Role modeling techniques)

32. **Correct Answer:** A. Advocate for the client's preferences even if they conflict with the family's wishes

    **Rationale:** In this situation, the social worker should advocate for the client's preferences because self-determination is a fundamental principle in social work and in end-of-life care. The client's right to make decisions about care should be respected, even if those decisions differ from the family's wishes. Encouraging the client to reconsider would undermine the client's autonomy by encouraging the client to align with the family's preferences, which may not respect the client's own values and wishes for end-of-life care. Facilitating a family meeting to mediate a compromise, which is valuable for addressing family dynamics, does not prioritize the client's right to self-determination. While a family meeting may be part of the process, the primary focus should remain on advocating for the client's expressed wishes. The correct answer must happen during a family meeting. This question calls for a single answer, not the ordering of several.

**Question Type:** Reasoning

**Content Area:** Professional Values and Ethics (Client/client system competence and self-determination [e.g., financial decisions, treatment decisions, emancipation, age of consent, permanency planning])

33. **Correct Answer:** B. Individual supervision

**Rationale:** Individual supervision is MOST appropriate when the supervisor is focusing on discussing challenging cases, providing detailed professional feedback, and identifying specific areas for improvement. This model allows for in-depth, personalized attention to each staff member's unique casework and professional development needs. It provides a private setting where the supervisor can address complex issues and offer tailored guidance that is directly relevant to the individual social worker's challenges and growth. Peer supervision involves staff members supporting and providing feedback to each other. While peer supervision can be valuable for sharing insights and learning collaboratively, it may not offer the structured, focused attention needed for addressing particularly challenging clients and detailed feedback on professional performance. Group supervision involves a supervisor meeting with a group of social workers and can be useful for collective problem-solving and sharing diverse perspectives. However, it often does not provide the same level of personalized feedback and detailed discussion on individual clients that individual supervision offers.

**Question Type:** Application

**Content Area:** Psychotherapy, Clinical Interventions, and Case Management (Models of supervision and consultation [e.g., individual, peer, group])

34. **Correct Answer:** A. Decreased tolerance levels

**Rationale:** When individuals relapse during recovery from substance use disorders, their tolerance levels are typically lower than before due to their period of abstinence. Consequently, using the same amount of a substance as previously can result in a higher relative dose, leading to an increased risk of overdose. The other options do not directly address the issue of how decreased tolerance contributes to overdose risk.

**Question Type:** Recall

**Content Area:** Human Development, Diversity, and Behavior in the Environment (Addiction theories and concepts)

35. **Correct Answer:** B. Collect detailed information from the client to identify the chronicity and severity of behaviors and symptoms

 **Rationale:** To accurately assess whether a client has co-occurring disorders, the social worker should FIRST collect detailed information to understand the chronicity and severity of both the substance use and mental health symptoms. This comprehensive assessment is crucial for identifying the extent of each disorder and how they may interact. While helping the client abstain from the substance so that the social worker can determine whether the mental health symptoms persist is important for treatment, it is not the first step in assessment. A thorough understanding of the client's symptoms and behaviors is needed before determining the effects of substance use cessation on mental health. Ruling out a substance use disorder without first understanding the full context of the client's symptoms can lead to incomplete assessment and treatment planning. A detailed assessment helps to integrate the understanding of both disorders.

 **Question Type:** Reasoning

 **Content Area:** Human Development, Diversity, and Behavior in the Environment (Co-occurring disorders and conditions)

36. **Correct Answer:** C. Prepare a list of goals and issues related to current work requirements

 **Rationale:** To BEST plan for a supervision session, the social worker should prepare a list of goals and issues related to current work requirements. This preparation ensures that the discussion is focused on relevant, immediate work challenges and objectives, allowing the supervisor to provide targeted feedback and support. It helps address specific concerns and aligns the session with the social worker's current professional needs. Reflecting on past challenges and successes is important but should complement the preparation of current work-related topics. Understanding agency policies is important but does not directly address the immediate needs related to the social worker's current job demands and professional development. It may be more suitable for a separate discussion or meeting focused specifically on agency policies.

**Question Type:** Application

**Content Area:** Professional Values and Ethics (Professional development activities to improve practice and maintain current professional knowledge [e.g., in-service training, licensing requirements, reviews of literature, workshops])

37. **Correct Answer:** B. Need for advanced medical treatments

**Rationale:** The level of care determination for nursing home admission focuses on whether the facility can meet the client's medical and support needs. A common reason for denial is that the client's need for advanced medical treatments or specialized care exceeds what the facility can provide. Nursing homes are equipped to handle certain levels of medical care, and if a client's needs surpass those capabilities, they may be denied admission. Nursing homes are specifically designed to assist with activities of daily living. This factor alone is unlikely to be the primary reason for denial unless combined with other, more complex care needs. Although staff shortages can affect the quality of care, the level of care determination primarily considers whether the facility's overall capabilities align with the client's medical needs rather than temporary staffing issues. Thus, the MOST likely factor for denying admission based on the level of care determination is the client's need for advanced medical treatments that exceed what the facility can offer.

**Question Type:** Reasoning

**Content Area:** Assessment, Diagnosis, and Treatment Planning (Placement options based on assessed level of care)

38. **Correct Answer:** A. Medication to manage symptoms

**Rationale:** DTs is a symptom associated with alcohol withdrawal that includes hallucinations, rapid respiration, temperature abnormalities, and body tremors. DTs is a severe condition resulting from alcohol withdrawal that requires immediate medical intervention. The MOST likely treatment for DTs is medication, specifically benzodiazepines, which help manage the acute withdrawal symptoms and stabilize the client's condition. Therapy for cravings and environmental restrictions are important for long-term recovery but are not the primary treatments for managing DTs.

**Question Type:** Application

**Content Area:** Human Development, Diversity, and Behavior in the Environment (Addiction theories and concepts)

39. **Correct Answer:** A. Review the licensure regulations in the jurisdiction

**Rationale:** To ensure eligibility for obtaining a necessary license, the social worker should review the licensure regulations in the jurisdiction in which practice will take place. This is crucial because licensure requirements can vary significantly by location, including specific educational qualifications, supervised experience, and examination requirements. Understanding these regulations ensures the social worker meets all criteria and avoids any potential issues with licensure. While consulting with the human resource department of the hiring agency or contacting the professional social work association might provide additional insights and guidance, reviewing the specific licensure regulations is the most direct way to confirm eligibility and ensure compliance with legal requirements for providing services. The social worker is ultimately responsible for complying with legal requirements for professional practice.

**Question Type:** Application

**Content Area:** Professional Values and Ethics (Legal and/or ethical issues related to the practice of social work, including responsibility to clients/client systems, colleagues, the profession, and society)

40. **Correct Answer:** C. Equifinality

**Rationale:** Equifinality refers to the principle that different causes or pathways can lead to the same outcome. In this scenario, despite the client's issues originating from different sources, they converge to produce similar negative effects. This BEST illustrates the concept of equifinality, where various factors result in the same end result.

**Question Type:** Application

**Content Area:** Human Development, Diversity, and Behavior in the Environment (Systems and ecological perspectives and theories)

41. **Correct Answer:** B. Role discomplementarity

**Rationale:** Role discomplementarity occurs when the roles and expectations of family members do not align or complement each other, leading to dysfunction or conflict. In the given scenario, the child is expected to assume responsibilities beyond the developmental level, while the parent is not effectively fulfilling a caregiving role. This misalignment in roles and expectations BEST reflects role discomplementarity in which the roles do not properly fit or support each other. Role confusion refers to a lack of clarity about one's role within a system, which is not specifically addressed in this scenario. Role strain involves difficulties in fulfilling the demands of a role, which may be related but does not capture the broader issue of misalignment between roles as clearly as role discomplementarity.

**Question Type:** Application

**Content Area:** Human Development, Diversity, and Behavior in the Environment (Role theories)

42. **Correct Answer:** B. Preoperational

**Rationale:** The child is MOST likely in the preoperational stage, which Piaget identifies as occurring between ages 2 and 7. In this stage, children often display egocentrism, as seen when the child insists that a toy truck can talk and becomes upset when others do not share this belief. They also show animism, attributing human traits to inanimate objects. Additionally, children in this stage struggle with the concept of conservation, which is reflected in the child's difficulty understanding that the truck cannot be in two places at once. The formal operational stage involves more advanced reasoning and abstract thinking, starting in adolescence, and the concrete operational stage involves logical thinking and understanding of conservation, which begins around age 7.

**Question Type:** Application

**Content Area:** Human Development, Diversity, and Behavior in the Environment (Theories of human development throughout the lifespan [e.g., physical, social, emotional, cognitive, behavioral])

43. **Correct Answer:** A. Social service eligibility considering the refugee status

**Rationale:** When assisting a refugee client, the primary consideration in locating services is determining eligibility for social services based on the refugee status. This includes understanding which services and programs the client qualifies for, which are specifically designed to address the unique needs of refugees, such as support for cultural adjustment, legal aid, and fiscal stability. While trauma-informed care is essential, the primary consideration for accessing services is ensuring the client meets eligibility criteria for various programs. Trauma-informed care will be important once eligibility is determined. Discrimination is a significant concern but does not directly impact the eligibility for social services. Addressing discrimination is important for the client's overall well-being, but eligibility for services is the primary factor in securing necessary assistance. Therefore, focusing on social service eligibility considering the refugee status is the most crucial factor when locating services for the client.

**Question Type:** Reasoning

**Content Area:** Assessment, Diagnosis, and Treatment Planning (The impact of immigration, refugee, or undocumented status on service delivery)

44. **Correct Answer:** A. Meet with each student individually to understand unique perspectives on the conflict

**Rationale:** Before attempting to resolve the conflict between the students, the social worker FIRST needs to gather information and understand the perspectives of each student involved. Meeting with each student individually allows the social worker to assess the underlying issues, emotions, and viewpoints contributing to the conflict. This step is crucial in developing a tailored and effective intervention strategy. Facilitating a joint meeting without this understanding could lead to further misunderstandings or escalation, while developing a classroom management plan addresses the broader issue of classroom disruption but does not directly resolve the conflict between the students.

**Question Type:** Reasoning

**Content Area:** Psychotherapy, Clinical Interventions, and Case Management (Methods of conflict resolution)

45. **Correct Answer:** A. Discuss ways to resolve the conflicts with the client

**Rationale:** When a social worker encounters a dual relationship, such as being a neighbor and attending the same community events as a client, the best approach is to discuss the situation openly with the client. This involves addressing any potential conflicts of interest or ethical concerns directly and collaboratively and finding ways to manage the dual relationship effectively. This approach helps maintain professional boundaries and ensure that the therapeutic relationship remains intact while addressing any issues that may arise from the dual relationship. Avoiding acknowledgment or discontinuing community activities may not address the underlying issues and could be less effective in managing the dual relationship professionally. Additionally, the incorrect response choices do not involve the client and resolving dual relationships must be handled collaboratively with the client. The social worker should not be the only one identifying the remedy.

**Question Type:** Reasoning

**Content Area:** Professional Values and Ethics (Ethical issues related to dual relationships)

46. **Correct Answer:** A. Discuss how the supervisee's client dynamics might be influencing behavior in supervision

**Rationale:** Parallel process occurs when the dynamics present in the supervisee's work with clients are mirrored in the supervisory relationship. For instance, if a client exhibits extreme dependency and the supervisee shows similar behaviors in supervision, this suggests that the patterns from the client relationship are affecting the supervisory dynamic. The supervisor should discuss how these client dynamics might influence the supervisee's behavior during supervision. This approach helps in understanding and managing the parallel process, enabling both the supervisor and supervisee to work through these issues and improve both client and supervisory relationships. Focusing solely on client work or suggesting outside support without addressing the parallel process may not fully address the underlying dynamics impacting the supervision.

**Question Type:** Reasoning

**Content Area:** Professional Values and Ethics (The impact of transference and countertransference within supervisory relationships)

47. **Correct Answer:** A. Reflect on how professional values and beliefs might be influencing perspectives and interactions within the team

    **Rationale:** Before addressing disagreements with team decisions or expressing frustration, it is crucial for the social worker to FIRST reflect on how professional values and beliefs might be influencing the social worker's perspectives and interactions. This self-reflection helps in understanding whether personal values are affecting the ability to collaborate effectively and impacts on client care. Recognizing these influences allows for a more informed and constructive approach to resolving conflicts. Expressing frustration or seeking supervision or consultation can be valuable steps, but they should follow an initial self-assessment to ensure that personal biases are not unduly shaping the approach to team dynamics.

    **Question Type:** Reasoning

    **Content Area:** Professional Values and Ethics (Professional objectivity in the social worker-client/client system relationship)

48. **Correct Answer:** C. Encourage the group to explore alternative approaches and critically evaluate each option

    **Rationale:** To BEST address concerns about groupthink and ensure a thorough evaluation of all options, the social worker should encourage the group to explore alternative approaches and critically evaluate each option. This approach helps to prevent decisions from being based solely on an unchallenged consensus and promotes a more comprehensive discussion of potential solutions. Simply agreeing with the group or gathering additional information does not directly address the risk of groupthink, whereas actively fostering diverse viewpoints and critical analysis helps ensure that the decision-making process remains objective and respectful of diverse viewpoints.

**Question Type:** Reasoning

**Content Area:** Professional Values and Ethics (Professional objectivity in the social worker-client/client system relationship)

49. **Correct Answer:** C. Arrange to check in with a supervisor or colleague before and after the visit

**Rationale:** When preparing for a home visit with a client who has a history of aggression, the social worker should arrange to check in with a supervisor or colleague before and after the visit. This approach ensures that there is a record of the social worker's whereabouts and provides contact with the agency in case any issues arise during the visit. Ensuring the address is noted is important but does not directly address the follow-up needed after the visit. Suggesting a public space can be a practical option but may not always be feasible or appropriate as the client may need a social worker to visit the home.

**Question Type:** Reasoning

**Content Area:** Professional Values and Ethics (Methods to create, implement, and evaluate policies and procedures for social worker safety)

50. **Correct Answer:** C. Conventional

**Rationale:** The adolescent's behavior MOST likely represents the conventional level of moral reasoning, where individuals follow societal norms and seek approval from others to maintain social order. At this stage, the youth's actions are motivated by the desire to fit in with peers and conform to expectations, which aligns with the conventional focus on upholding societal rules and roles. In contrast, the preconventional level is centered around avoiding punishment and seeking personal gain, which does not fully capture the peer-influenced behavior described. The postconventional level involves principles of justice and ethical reasoning beyond societal norms, which is not reflected in the described focus on peer conformity.

**Question Type:** Application

**Content Area:** Human Development, Diversity, and Behavior in the Environment (Theories of human development throughout the lifespan [e.g., physical, social, emotional, cognitive, behavioral])

51. **Correct Answer:** B. Lean forward slightly to convey interest and empathy

**Rationale:** Leaning forward slightly is a powerful nonverbal communication technique that signals the social worker's engagement, interest, and empathy during difficult discussions. This gesture helps convey that the social worker is actively listening and invested in the client's experience, which can encourage the client to feel more comfortable and open up about challenging topics. While maintaining eye contact is important, too much eye contact can sometimes feel intimidating or intense, especially when discussing difficult topics. The social worker should balance eye contact with other nonverbal cues. Additionally, eye contact often has cultural considerations. Nodding is a positive reinforcement technique, but on its own, it may not be enough to address the client's withdrawal during difficult conversations. The client is not speaking, so nodding is awkward as it is usually used when a social worker is agreeing with what is being said.

**Question Type:** Reasoning

**Content Area:** Psychotherapy, Clinical Interventions, and Case Management (Verbal and nonverbal communication techniques)

52. **Correct Answer:** C. Reviewing progress and anticipating future needs based on the prognosis

**Rationale:** The MOST important part of the discharge process is ensuring that the client's progress is thoroughly reviewed and that future needs are anticipated based on the client's prognosis. This helps to create a tailored discharge plan that addresses any ongoing challenges and prepares the client for the transition from residential care to independent living or other levels of care. With this focus, the social worker ensures that the client can have continued success and that any potential issues are identified and planned for in advance. Simply providing resources does not guarantee the client will know how or when to access them. The client should have a clear understanding of the protocols needed before the discharge process as this understanding should be the basis of intervention.

**Question Type:** Recall

**Content Area:** Assessment, Diagnosis, and Treatment Planning (Discharge, aftercare, and follow-up planning)

53. **Correct Answer:** B. Giving extra chores to a child who broke a rule

**Rationale:** Positive punishment involves adding an undesirable consequence to reduce the likelihood of a behavior being repeated. In this case, giving extra chores is the BEST example of positive punishment because it adds an additional task as a consequence for the child's behavior. Removing a toy is an example of negative punishment as it involves taking away a privilege to decrease unwanted behavior. Ignoring the behavior is a form of extinction and not related to positive punishment.

**Question Type:** Application

**Content Area:** Human Development, Diversity, and Behavior in the Environment (Theories of human development throughout the lifespan [e.g., physical, social, emotional, cognitive, behavioral])

54. **Correct Answer:** C. Identify realistic goals for improvement which include more opportunities for practice

    **Rationale:** Setting realistic goals for improvement and providing more opportunities for practice are crucial for helping the client progress. This approach offers clear, actionable steps for the client to work on, which can BEST enhance skills and understanding. While highlighting efforts and progress is important for encouragement, it does not directly address the need for structured improvement and practice. Revisiting previous lessons may be beneficial but is less focused on creating a forward-looking plan for continued development.

    **Question Type:** Reasoning

    **Content Area:** Psychotherapy, Clinical Interventions, and Case Management (Methods to obtain and provide feedback)

55. **Correct Answer:** B. Increase client awareness and control of physiological functions

    **Rationale:** The PRIMARY goal of biofeedback is to help clients gain awareness of and control over physiological functions, such as heart rate, muscle tension, or skin temperature. This process allows individuals to learn how to regulate these physiological processes to manage stress, improve health, and enhance overall well-being.

    **Question Type:** Recall

    **Content Area:** Human Development, Diversity, and Behavior in the Environment (Theories of human development throughout the lifespan [e.g., physical, social, emotional, cognitive, behavioral])

56. **Correct Answer:** B. Provide immediate support to address the client's housing and financial needs

    **Rationale:** In a crisis intervention approach, the primary focus is on providing immediate support to stabilize the client's situation and address urgent needs. In this scenario, the social worker should prioritize helping the client with immediate housing and financial needs, such as arranging temporary shelter and connecting them with emergency resources. This approach ensures that the client's immediate safety and basic needs are met, which is crucial in managing acute emotional distress. Assisting with future goal setting and exploring past trauma are important but should come after addressing the immediate crisis and stabilizing the client's situation. Additionally, there is no information about the setting in which the social worker is employed. Exploring past trauma may not be appropriate if the social worker works for an emergency relief organization as the social worker will be working with the client for a limited time period.

**Question Type:** Reasoning

**Content Area:** Psychotherapy, Clinical Interventions, and Case Management (Crisis intervention and treatment approaches)

57. **Correct Answer:** A. Practice specific anger management techniques together during meetings

**Rationale:** Practicing specific anger management techniques together during sessions is the BEST method for teaching the client because it provides hands-on experience and immediate feedback. This approach allows the social worker to model the techniques, demonstrate their application in real time, and help the client practice them in a supportive environment. This interactive process helps the client understand and integrate the techniques into daily life more effectively. Referring the client to a support group and encouraging journaling are valuable supplementary strategies, but they do not offer the same level of direct instruction and practice that working together in sessions provides. Additionally, a social worker is not assisting with anger management if the client is learning via a support group; the support group is the change agent. Understanding the triggers does not mean that the client will be able to employ necessary techniques for effective management.

**Question Type:** Reasoning

**Content Area:** Psychotherapy, Clinical Interventions, and Case Management (Anger management techniques)

58. **Correct Answer:** C. Conduct a safety assessment to ensure the client's well-being

**Rationale:** Conducting a safety assessment is the FIRST priority to address any potential risks to the client's well-being, given the multiple crises and high levels of distress. This step ensures that the client's safety and mental health are secured before addressing other issues. Referring the client to emergency assistance and exploring coping skills are important but come after ensuring the client is safe. Addressing financial stability or coping skills without first assessing and ensuring the client's immediate safety could overlook critical risks and exacerbate the client's situation. This approach is consistent with the hierarchy of needs.

**Question Type:** Reasoning

**Content Area:** Human Development, Diversity, and Behavior in the Environment (Basic human needs)

59. **Correct Answer:** A. Identifying dynamic risk factors

**Rationale:** Identifying dynamic risk factors is the MOST important aspect of the risk assessment process for guiding immediate intervention. Dynamic risk factors are those that can change over time and are often related to the current state of the client's mental health, such as recent changes in behavior, mood, or circumstances. By focusing on these factors, the social worker can identify immediate threats to the client's safety and adjust interventions accordingly. Increasing knowledge about static risk factors is less relevant for immediate intervention because static risk factors are fixed and unchangeable, such as past trauma or genetic predispositions. While understanding these factors is important for comprehensive risk assessment, they do not directly guide immediate intervention. Knowing the available community-based crisis resources is crucial for providing support and resources, but it is secondary to identifying the current risk factors that need immediate attention. Understanding the client's dynamic risk factors helps determine what kind of resources and interventions will be most effective in the short term.

**Question Type:** Reasoning

**Content Area:** Assessment, Diagnosis, and Treatment Planning (Risk assessment methods)

60. **Correct Answer:** C. Encourage self-determination

**Rationale:** Encouraging self-determination is crucial when working with older adults as it empowers them to make their own choices and maintain control over their lives despite aging-related challenges. This response choice also serves as "an umbrella option" because it can encompass goals related to both physical health and social relationships. By focusing on self-determination, the social worker helps the client address health issues and social isolation while supporting overall autonomy and well-being. While managing medical treatments and enhancing social relationships are important aspects, self-determination provides a comprehensive framework that integrates both elements, promoting a holistic approach to the client's needs.

**Question Type:** Reasoning

**Content Area:** Human Development, Diversity, and Behavior in the Environment (The effect of aging on biopsychosocial functioning)

61. **Correct Answer:** C. Facilitate the client's participation in an advocacy group to become a change agent

    **Rationale:** Facilitating the client's participation in an advocacy group is the BEST way to empower because it helps the client engage in broader systemic change and become an active agent in shaping the environment. This macro-level approach provides the client with a sense of purpose and agency by involving the client in activities that influence community and support collective efforts. It enhances confidence and reinforces the ability to make impactful changes. While helping the client set short-term, achievable goals and assisting in understanding how current actions impact the future are important for personal development, the social worker is more focused on individual behavior rather than enabling the client to influence larger systems and communities, which is the basis of an empowerment approach.

    **Question Type:** Application

    **Content Area:** Psychotherapy, Clinical Interventions, and Case Management (Strengths-based and empowerment strategies and interventions)

62. **Correct Answer:** C. Identify and prioritize the smaller, manageable components of the problem

    **Rationale:** The FIRST step in partializing a problem is to identify and prioritize the smaller, more manageable components of the issue. This approach allows the social worker and client to break down a complex problem into specific parts that can be addressed individually. By doing so, the problem becomes less overwhelming, and the client can focus on tackling each component systematically. Assessing the client's readiness and reviewing past experiences are important steps that follow after the problem has been broken down and prioritized. These steps help tailor the intervention to the client's needs and previous coping strategies, but the initial focus should be on dividing the problem into manageable parts. The social worker cannot assess the client's readiness if the steps are not yet identified. Reviewing past experiences is also not directly related to partialization which is the content assessed by this question.

    **Question Type:** Recall

    **Content Area:** Psychotherapy, Clinical Interventions, and Case Management (Partializing techniques)

63. **Correct Answer:** B. Explore with the client how negative beliefs about body image are linked to self-esteem

    **Rationale:** Exploring with the client how negative beliefs about body image are linked to self-esteem is the BEST approach as it addresses the underlying issues contributing to the client's negative body image. By examining and challenging these beliefs, the social worker can help the client improve self-esteem and develop a healthier self-image. Helping the client to understand that physical appearance should not be judged does not tackle the client's internal struggles or provide a therapeutic strategy, while assuring the client, although empathetic, does not offer a solution to the client's specific issues with body image and self-esteem.

    **Question Type:** Reasoning

    **Content Area:** Human Development, Diversity, and Behavior in the Environment (Body image and its impact [e.g., identity, self-esteem, relationships, habits])

64. **Correct Answer:** A. Conduct a motivational interviewing session with the client

    **Rationale:** The most effective FIRST step when a client expresses interest in making a change, especially in the context of substance use, is to engage in a motivational interviewing (MI) session. MI is a client-centered approach designed to enhance motivation and commitment to change by exploring and resolving ambivalence. It is particularly effective in helping clients recognize their readiness to change, set goals, and develop a plan for action. Referring the client to a support group is an important step in the overall treatment process but is not the first action. There is no indication that the client has any physical concerns, so asking the client to see a physician is also not needed. Before taking these steps, it is crucial to understand the client's motivation and readiness for change through MI. This allows the social worker to tailor the subsequent interventions to the client's needs and ensure that the client is fully engaged in the process.

    **Question Type:** Reasoning

    **Content Area:** Assessment, Diagnosis, and Treatment Planning (Methods to assess motivation, resistance, and readiness to change)

65. **Correct Answer:** B. Inform both parties about the subpoena and consult with legal counsel

    **Rationale:** To handle the situation ethically, the social worker should inform both parties about the subpoena and consult with legal counsel. This ensures that the social worker's response is legally sound and considers the ethical implications of disclosing confidential information. Consulting with legal counsel provides guidance on how to navigate the subpoena while maintaining compliance with legal and ethical standards. Simply complying with the subpoena or claiming privilege without proper legal advice may not fully address the complexities involved in protecting client confidentiality and managing legal obligations.

**Question Type:** Reasoning

**Content Area:** Professional Values and Ethics (Legal and/or ethical issues regarding confidentiality, including electronic information security)

66. **Correct Answer:** B. Explore how the client's environment and family dynamics impact overall well-being

    **Rationale:** Using an ecological perspective involves examining how various aspects of a client's environment, including family dynamics, job stress, and access to community resources, interact and affect overall well-being. This approach helps in understanding the interconnected nature of the client's problems and how they influence each other. While addressing immediate concerns and prioritizing issues are important, the ecological perspective emphasizes the need to look at the broader context and the interactions between different life domains.

    **Question Type:** Reasoning

    **Content Area:** Human Development, Diversity, and Behavior in the Environment (Systems and ecological perspectives and theories)

67. **Correct Answer:** B. Implement a behavior management plan to help the child manage the disruptive behaviors

    **Rationale:** A behavior management plan is the BEST intervention in this situation because the primary concern is the child's disruptive behaviors in school and at home. The client is the child, not the parents. By implementing a behavior management plan, the social worker can help the child develop better coping mechanisms, reduce outbursts, and improve the ability to follow instructions. While therapy and psychoeducation are important, the immediate need is to address disruptive behaviors directly.

    **Question Type:** Reasoning

    **Content Area:** Assessment, Diagnosis, and Treatment Planning (The criteria used in the selection of intervention/treatment modalities [e.g., client/client system abilities, culture, life stage])

68. **Correct Answer:** B. Disrupt the current dysfunctional patterns to encourage the family to think about the adolescent's behavior differently

    **Rationale:** Disrupting the dysfunctional patterns is correct because, in strategic family therapy, a paradoxical directive is MOST often used to prompt the family to reconsider and alter their approach to a problem. By encouraging the parents to intentionally increase the adolescent's defiant behavior, the social worker aims to highlight the unproductive nature of current strategies and encourage a shift in how the family perceives and handles the adolescent's behavior. The primary goal of the paradoxical directive is not to empower the adolescent or give the adolescent more control. Additionally, the family is the client, not the adolescent, so the intervention needs to be focused on the family. The paradoxical directive is not intended to provide a structured way for the adolescent to express frustrations or decrease the frequency of arguments directly. Instead, its intent is to challenge the family's current approach to conflict and encourage new ways of thinking and interacting.

    **Question Type:** Application

    **Content Area:** Psychotherapy, Clinical Interventions, and Case Management (Family therapy models, interventions, and approaches)

69. **Correct Answer:** C. Developing and implementing a behavioral intervention plan to address the child's behavioral challenges

    **Rationale:** Addressing the child's behavioral challenges is a crucial step in permanency planning. Behavioral issues can impact a child's ability to be successfully placed in a stable, long-term home. By developing and implementing a behavioral intervention plan, the social worker helps to address these challenges, which can improve the likelihood of a successful permanency plan by making the child more suitable for a permanent placement. While monitoring academic progress is important, it does not directly address the child's behavioral issues that are influencing placement stability. Facilitating meetings with potential adoptive or permanent guardians is part of the permanency process, but addressing behavioral issues directly through intervention is MOST important for ensuring the child is prepared for a successful placement.

    **Question Type:** Reasoning

    **Content Area:** Psychotherapy, Clinical Interventions, and Case Management (Permanency planning)

70. **Correct Answer:** A. Schedule a time to speak with the client to determine the nature of the existing problem

**Rationale:** The most appropriate action is to schedule a time to speak with the former client to understand the nature of the new issue. There is no ethical prohibition against serving a former client. However, the client's current need may be beyond the social worker's expertise so more information is needed from the client. This information can be obtained during a conversation with the client. Consulting agency policy is not appropriate as the question calls for addressing the situation ethically and ethical standards can conflict with agency policy. Additionally, suggesting the client find another provider means that a client has to engage and develop rapport with another professional, which may not be needed. Reengaging with the social worker may be appropriate if the social worker is competent to address this new unrelated issue.

**Question Type:** Reasoning

**Content Area:** Professional Values and Ethics (Legal and/or ethical issues regarding termination)

71. **Correct Answer:** B. Decline the referral as incentive payments are not allowed

**Rationale:** The ethical issue in this scenario is the presence of incentive payments for referrals, which can create conflicts of interest and potentially affect the objectivity of the social worker's decision-making. To address this situation ethically, the social worker should decline the referral to avoid any involvement with incentive payments that might compromise professional integrity. With incentive payments, the focus may shift from client needs to financial gain. This undermines trust and ethical standards in client care. Meeting with the family does not address the ethical concern related to the financial incentives and could unintentionally begin the process that may conflict with ethical guidelines. Ensuring adherence to ethical standards involves avoiding situations where financial incentives could influence professional decisions.

**Question Type:** Reasoning

**Content Area:** Professional Values and Ethics (Legal and/or ethical issues related to the practice of social work, including responsibility to clients/client systems, colleagues, the profession, and society)

72. **Correct Answer:** A. Confront the colleague directly about the behavior so that remedial action can be taken

**Rationale:** According to ethical guidelines, the social worker should FIRST address the issue directly with the colleague. This approach respects the colleague's autonomy and provides an opportunity to discuss and resolve the behavior in a supportive manner. Confronting the colleague directly or calling attention to the behavior allows the colleague to be aware of the impact of the actions and to take corrective measures. Reporting the issue to a supervisor or providing resources may be appropriate if the behavior continues, but addressing it directly aligns with ethical practices of attempting to resolve conflicts with the involved parties. Also, providing resources, while supportive, does not mean that the colleague recognizes the impact of the caregiving on professional practice, so change may not occur.

**Question Type:** Reasoning

**Content Area:** Professional Values and Ethics (Legal and/or ethical issues regarding mandatory reporting [e.g., abuse, threat of harm, impaired professionals, etc.])

73. **Correct Answer:** A. Help the client identify past successes which have resulted in resilience

**Rationale:** Using a strength-based approach involves focusing on the client's strengths and past successes to build resilience and address current challenges. By helping the client recognize previous accomplishments and how they have overcome difficulties in the past, the social worker can empower the client to draw on these strengths to manage the current situation. This approach contrasts with exploring reasons for frustration or providing immediate external support, which may not directly foster the client's own capacity for resilience and self-efficacy.

**Question Type:** Reasoning

**Content Area:** Human Development, Diversity, and Behavior in the Environment (Strengths-based and resilience theories)

74. **Correct Answer:** A. Client smiles while expressing feelings of happiness during a session.

**Rationale:** Congruence in communication occurs when a person's verbal expression is aligned with the person's nonverbal cues. The client smiling while expressing feelings of happiness BEST demonstrates that the emotional expression matches the client's verbal communication, demonstrating congruence. Using a neutral tone may not fully convey the client's feelings about an accomplishment, indicating potential incongruence. Avoiding eye contact when discussing a breach of trust might suggest discomfort but does not necessarily indicate congruence between verbal and nonverbal communication.

**Question Type:** Reasoning

**Content Area:** Assessment, Diagnosis, and Treatment Planning (Methods to assess motivation, resistance, and readiness to change)

75. **Correct Answer:** B. Clarify the client's presenting problem

**Rationale:** To engage effectively in problem formulation, the social worker should FIRST clarify the client's presenting problem. This involves gathering detailed information about the client's difficulties to understand the nature and scope of the issues. Accurately defining the problem is crucial for developing an appropriate intervention plan. While praising the client for seeking help is supportive, it does not contribute to the formulation of the problem. Focusing on solutions before fully understanding the presenting problems can lead to ineffective or misaligned interventions. The primary focus should be on understanding and clarifying the issues first.

**Question Type:** Reasoning

**Content Area:** Assessment, Diagnosis, and Treatment Planning (The factors and processes used in problem formulation)

76. **Correct Answer:** A. Social workers should conduct internet searches only when it is essential to client safety.

**Rationale:** Social work standards dictate that internet searches for client information should be conducted only when necessary for compelling professional reasons and, when appropriate, with client consent. However, in order to ensure client safety, social workers may act without appropriate informed consent. This approach BEST balances the need for information with respect for client privacy and confidentiality. Gathering information without consent should not be done indiscriminately, and there should not be a complete avoidance of internet searches if there are danger or safety concerns. Both incorrect response choices do not align with ethical standards that permit searches without consent only under specific, safety-related circumstances.

**Question Type:** Recall

**Content Area:** Professional Values and Ethics (The principles and processes of obtaining informed consent)

77. **Correct Answer:** B. Gain a clearer understanding of the client's challenges

**Rationale:** Collateral informants are used to gather additional perspectives and insights that can provide a more comprehensive view of a client's difficulties. In this scenario, consulting the client's spouse and employer MOST likely helps the social worker gain a fuller picture of the client's struggles with anxiety and its impact on employment and relationships. This broader perspective aids in forming a more accurate assessment and creating a more effective treatment plan. While validating the client's self-reported symptoms can be a function of using collaterals, there is no indication in the scenario that the client is unreliable. Additionally, the need to assess the strength of support systems is also not indicated in the question.

**Question Type:** Reasoning

**Content Area:** Assessment, Diagnosis, and Treatment Planning (Methods of involving clients/client systems in problem identification [e.g., gathering collateral information])

78. **Correct Answer:** B. Mindfulness

**Rationale:** The technique described, where the social worker encourages the client to focus on the present moment and increase awareness of thoughts and feelings, is known as mindfulness. Mindfulness practices are specifically designed to help individuals become more aware of and accept current experiences, which can reduce feelings of overwhelm associated with stress and anxiety. Cognitive restructuring involves changing negative thought patterns and is a different approach to managing stress. Relaxation exercises focus on reducing physical symptoms of stress but do not directly address increasing awareness of the present moment like mindfulness does.

**Question Type:** Application

**Content Area:** Psychotherapy, Clinical Interventions, and Case Management (Mindfulness and complementary therapeutic approaches)

79. **Correct Answer:** C. Impact of the illness on biopsychosocial functioning

**Rationale:** When a client is diagnosed with a chronic illness, the social worker should FIRST focus on understanding how the illness affects the client's overall biopsychosocial functioning. This approach allows the social worker to assess how the illness impacts the client's emotional well-being, daily life, and social interactions. By evaluating the biopsychosocial impact, the social worker can better identify areas where the client might need support and tailor interventions to address these comprehensive needs. Addressing the broader impact is crucial for developing a holistic treatment plan, whereas focusing solely on physical illness management may overlook critical aspects of the client's experience. The need for coping skills and supports is important but can only be determined after the impacts of the illness are understood, so this focus is not first.

**Question Type:** Reasoning

**Content Area:** Assessment, Diagnosis, and Treatment Planning (Biopsychosocial responses to illness and disability)

80. **Correct Answer:** B. Lower economic mobility

**Rationale:** Prolonged exposure to discrimination MOST likely leads to lower economic mobility, as it often results in fewer opportunities for advancement in employment and education, which directly affects financial stability and career growth. Although discrimination can also impact mental health and social integration, the long-term and systemic effects of discrimination are most closely related to economic challenges. Both education and employment are linked to financial mobility but may have less impact on social integration and mental health as the question does not mention discrimination in other life areas.

**Question Type:** Application

**Content Area:** Human Development, Diversity, and Behavior in the Environment (The effects of discrimination and stereotypes on behaviors, attitudes, and identity)

81. **Correct Answer:** B. Conscious self-concept and self-esteem

**Rationale:** According to ego psychology, understanding a client's behavior that includes defensive reactions and an inflated sense of self-importance is MOST relevant to examining conscious self-concept and self-esteem. Ego psychology focuses on the ways in which individuals perceive and maintain their self-identity and self-worth in the present moment. The client's defensive behaviors and grandiosity are often reflections of client self-esteem. Unresolved unconscious conflicts are often related to a psychodynamic approach and Freud studied how early childhood experiences can influence behavior, but this work is not the basis of ego psychology.

**Question Type:** Application

**Content Area:** Psychotherapy, Clinical Interventions, and Case Management (Psychoanalytic and psychodynamic approaches)

82. **Correct Answer:** B. Broker

**Rationale:** In case management, the role of a broker is MOST effective for assisting clients. A broker helps connect clients with necessary services and resources, coordinating and facilitating access to various supports. This role is critical in managing and navigating the complex network of services and ensuring clients receive the comprehensive care they need. While advocacy and mediation are valuable roles, the broker role specifically focuses on the practical aspect of linking clients with the appropriate resources and services.

**Question Type:** Recall

**Content Area:** Psychotherapy, Clinical Interventions, and Case Management (The components of case management)

83. **Correct Answer:** C. Help the community prioritize policies and practices that are inherently biased

**Rationale:** Addressing systemic discrimination effectively requires first identifying and understanding the specific policies and practices that contribute to inequality. By prioritizing and addressing these inherently biased elements, the social worker can create a foundation for more targeted and effective interventions. While developing legal advocacy services and advocating for policy changes are important, they are more effective when informed by a clear understanding of the core issues and are not done before prioritization which is part of planning. Focusing on identifying and addressing the biased policies and practices FIRST ensures that subsequent efforts are grounded in addressing the root causes of the discrimination.

**Question Type:** Reasoning

**Content Area:** Human Development, Diversity, and Behavior in the Environment (Systemic [institutionalized] discrimination [e.g., racism, sexism, ageism])

84. **Correct Answer:** A. Hematuria

**Rationale:** Hematuria, the presence of blood in the urine, is a potentially serious medical symptom that could indicate an underlying health condition requiring immediate attention, such as a urinary tract infection, kidney stones, or even more severe issues like bladder or kidney cancer. Addressing hematuria FIRST is essential to ensure that any serious medical conditions are identified and treated promptly, which is critical before focusing on the client's other concerns, such as job instability or apathy. Prioritizing physical health is necessary to ensure the client is stable and can engage effectively in addressing other psychosocial issues.

**Question Type:** Reasoning

**Content Area:** Assessment, Diagnosis, and Treatment Planning (Basic medical terminology)

85. **Correct Answer:** B. Systemic economic disparities that served as institutional barriers

**Rationale:** Systemic economic disparities and institutional barriers are the MOST likely causes of widespread issues such as inadequate housing, limited access to healthcare, and unemployment in impoverished communities. These systemic factors create and perpetuate conditions of inequality and poverty. Increased gentrification can contribute to economic decline but is less directly related to the root causes of these problems. Lack of engagement might be a consequence rather than a primary cause of the issues faced by the community. Addressing systemic economic disparities is essential for addressing the fundamental challenges faced by impoverished communities.

**Question Type:** Application

**Content Area:** Human Development, Diversity, and Behavior in the Environment (The effect of poverty on individuals, families, groups, organizations, and communities)

86. **Correct Answer:** A. Speaking directly to community members to hear their experiences with the policy

**Rationale:** The MOST important activity for the social worker in this scenario is speaking directly to community members to hear their experiences with the policy. Engaging with the affected community provides firsthand insights into how the policy is functioning on the ground, whether it meets the needs of the population, and any barriers they might face. This qualitative data is crucial for understanding the real-world impact of the policy. While examining utilization rates and ensuring economic and social access are considered important aspects of a comprehensive analysis, the direct feedback from the community offers valuable context that numbers and statistics alone cannot provide.

**Question Type:** Reasoning

**Content Area:** Psychotherapy, Clinical Interventions, and Case Management (The effects of policies, procedures, regulations, and legislation on social work practice and service delivery)

87. **Correct Answer:** A. Organize town hall meetings so residents can voice their concerns and propose solutions

**Rationale:** The FIRST step the social worker should take to mobilize community participation is to organize town hall meetings. This approach allows residents to come together, express their concerns, and propose solutions in an open and collaborative environment. It fosters a sense of community ownership and engagement, which is essential for building momentum and collective action. While developing a survey and forming a coalition are important strategies, starting with town hall meetings ensures that the community's voices are heard directly and immediately, creating a foundation for further participation and initiatives. Additionally, there is benefit from residents hearing the diversity of perspectives and the information generated from the town halls may assist with shaping the questions for the survey. Coalition formation should occur after the problems are identified and solutions prioritized.

**Question Type:** Reasoning

**Content Area:** Psychotherapy, Clinical Interventions, and Case Management (Techniques for mobilizing community participation)

88. **Correct Answer:** C. Means testing

    **Rationale:** Means testing is a process used to determine whether an individual or family qualifies for government assistance programs, including subsidized housing. It involves assessing the client's financial resources, income, and assets to determine if they meet the eligibility criteria for the subsidy. A mental status examination and biopsychosocial assessment are important tools in understanding the client's overall mental health and social functioning, but they are not directly relevant to determining eligibility for subsidized housing. Means testing is MOST helpful as this assessment directly relates to the financial criteria required for such housing assistance.

    **Question Type:** Application

    **Content Area:** Assessment, Diagnosis, and Treatment Planning (Techniques and instruments used to assess clients/client systems)

89. **Correct Answer:** C. Ask the group to evaluate its interconnected relationships

    **Rationale:** The BEST way for the social worker to strengthen group cohesion is to ask the group to evaluate its interconnected relationships. By encouraging members to reflect on how they relate to one another, the social worker can help the group identify and address dynamics that may be contributing to distance or hesitation. This process promotes a deeper understanding of the group as a whole, leading to stronger connections and a more cohesive group environment. While reviewing group goals and encouraging sharing are important, focusing on the relationships within the group directly targets the underlying factors that influence cohesion.

    **Question Type:** Reasoning

    **Content Area:** Psychotherapy, Clinical Interventions, and Case Management (Group work techniques and approaches [e.g., developing and managing group processes and cohesion])

90. **Correct Answer:** C. Serve as a support broker for the client during the process

    **Rationale:** Serving as a support broker is the most comprehensive approach for assisting the client. This role not only involves connecting the client with necessary resources and services but also incorporates elements of exploring gender identity and providing information about medical procedures. By acting as a support broker, the social worker addresses both the emotional and practical challenges the client faces, making it "an umbrella option" that encompasses and integrates aspects of the other two response choices as the client might need both emotional and practical support.

**Question Type:** Application

**Content Area:** Human Development, Diversity, and Behavior in the Environment (The impact of transgender and transitioning process on behaviors, attitudes, identity, and relationships)

91. **Correct Answer:** B. Provision of a supportive environment that respects the client's emotional needs

**Rationale:** The MOST important aspect of supporting a client who is transitioning to another gender is providing a supportive environment that respects the client's emotional needs. This approach is crucial because it helps the client navigate the emotional and psychological challenges associated with transitioning. While knowledge about gender-affirming medical interventions and consideration of the client's intersectionality with other LGBTQI+ identities are valuable, they are secondary to creating an environment that offers emotional support and validation, which is fundamental to the client's overall well-being during the transition process.

**Question Type:** Recall

**Content Area:** Human Development, Diversity, and Behavior in the Environment (The impact of transgender and transitioning process on behaviors, attitudes, identity, and relationships)

92. **Correct Answer:** A. Accept the gift with an expression of gratitude

**Rationale:** Gift giving is not prohibited by ethical standards but can create a conflict of interest or blurred boundaries. In cases where a gift is given at the end of a therapeutic relationship, it is generally acceptable to accept it with gratitude, especially when the gift is modest and given as a token of appreciation. This approach recognizes the client's gesture of thanks while maintaining a professional and respectful closure to the relationship. However, it is important to consider the context and agency policies. There is no ethical standard that mandates declining homemade gifts and the social worker sharing with others is irrelevant as the question asks about the appropriateness of accepting.

**Question Type:** Reasoning

**Content Area:** Professional Values and Ethics (Legal and/or ethical issues related to the practice of social work, including responsibility to clients/client systems, colleagues, the profession, and society)

93. **Correct Answer:** A. Offering relapse prevention programs for individuals in recovery

**Rationale:** Tertiary prevention focuses on managing and mitigating the impact of an existing condition by preventing further deterioration and supporting recovery. In this scenario, offering relapse prevention programs for individuals in recovery is a tertiary prevention activity because it helps those already affected by substance use disorders to maintain their progress and avoid future relapses. Screening high-risk populations is a secondary prevention activity aimed at early detection to prevent substance use, while advocating for policies that limit access to addictive substances is a primary prevention strategy that seeks to prevent the onset of substance use.

**Question Type:** Application

**Content Area:** Psychotherapy, Clinical Interventions, and Case Management (Primary, secondary, and tertiary prevention strategies)

94. **Correct Answer:** B. Advocate that the client meet with human resources personnel to discuss this request

**Rationale:** The BEST approach is for the social worker to advocate for the client to engage with human resources. This step allows the client to address the issue directly with the employer and explore potential accommodations or solutions that respect her religious practices. While informing the client about discriminatory practices and seeking alternative employment are also important considerations, working through the proper channels in the workplace is the most immediate and effective way to address and resolve the situation.

**Question Type:** Reasoning

**Content Area:** Human Development, Diversity, and Behavior in the Environment (The effects of discrimination and stereotypes on behaviors, attitudes, and identity)

95. **Correct Answer:** C. Ask the client to describe a recent conversation or event

**Rationale:** Asking the client to describe a recent conversation or event is the most effective FIRST step for assessing communication skills because it provides immediate insight into the ability to articulate thoughts and reflect on communication experiences. This approach allows the social worker to understand the client's challenges with expressing needs and interpreting social interactions in a practical context. Observations in group settings or using formal testing tools can be valuable later but may not directly address the client's specific difficulties at the beginning of the assessment as they take time and do not provide immediate information.

**Question Type:** Application

**Content Area:** Assessment, Diagnosis, and Treatment Planning (Methods to assess the client's/client system's communication skills)

96. **Correct Answer:** C. Gather feedback from participants and staff to make real-time improvements

    **Rationale:** A formative evaluation is conducted during the early or ongoing stages of a program to assess how well it is being implemented and to make necessary adjustments. By gathering feedback from participants and staff, the social worker can identify any issues or areas for improvement as the program progresses, allowing for real-time modifications that enhance the program's effectiveness. Comparing participant outcomes to those of youth who were not in the program and ensuring that participants represent youth in the broader community are important considerations but are not the primary focus of a formative evaluation.

    **Question Type:** Application

    **Content Area:** Assessment, Diagnosis, and Treatment Planning (Methods, techniques, and instruments used to evaluate social work practice)

97. **Correct Answer:** B. Integrating client preferences and values with the appropriate evidence-based practice

    **Rationale:** The BEST approach when selecting an intervention strategy is to integrate client preferences and values with the appropriate evidence-based practice. This method ensures that the chosen interventions are not only supported by research but also align with the client's individual needs, preferences, and values. This approach promotes a collaborative process where both empirical evidence and the client's personal context are considered, leading to more effective and personalized care. Relying solely on the social worker's expertise or asking the client to identify the protocols does not adequately address the need for integrating research evidence with client-centered considerations.

    **Question Type:** Application

    **Content Area:** Professional Values and Ethics (Evidence-based practice)

98. **Correct Answer:** B. Provide the parents with a list of other qualified providers instead of directly providing services

**Rationale:** Engaging in a therapeutic relationship with close friends or their family members can create a dual relationship, which may lead to ethical conflicts and compromised professional boundaries. By referring the adolescent to another qualified provider, the social worker ensures that the child receives unbiased and objective care while maintaining the integrity of both the professional relationship and the personal friendship. This approach adheres to ethical standards and helps avoid any potential conflicts of interest. Providing therapy to a close friend's child can blur professional boundaries and lead to dual relationships, which are ethically problematic. The social worker's objectivity and professional judgment could be compromised by the preexisting personal relationship, which can impact the quality of care provided. Asking the parents for more details about the adolescent's problems may deepen the involvement in the situation and potentially increase pressure to provide services, further complicating the ethical dilemma. Instead, it is more appropriate to maintain professional boundaries from the outset by referring them to another provider.

**Question Type:** Reasoning

**Content Area:** Professional Values and Ethics (Ethical issues related to dual relationships)

99. **Correct Answer:** A. Seek consultation from professional colleagues

**Rationale:** When a social worker encounters a treatment-resistant problem and remains uncertain about next steps despite reviewing relevant literature, seeking consultation from professional colleagues is the most effective course of action. Colleagues can provide additional perspectives, share their own experiences, and offer new strategies or interventions that may not have been considered. Asking the client for insight might not yield actionable solutions if the treatment is resistant. While involving the client in discussions can be valuable, asking the client to provide insight into why interventions are not effective might not always yield useful or actionable information. Clients may not have the expertise or knowledge to identify why specific interventions are not working, especially in complex or treatment-resistant cases. The client's feedback might be limited to personal experience without addressing underlying clinical or methodological issues that need expert analysis. Lastly, referring the client to another social worker may not address the immediate need for expert advice and collaboration to resolve the issue effectively. If the client goes to a new social worker, the entire problem-solving process has to begin again, starting with engagement. This action should not be done NEXT.

**Question Type:** Reasoning

**Content Area:** Psychotherapy, Clinical Interventions, and Case Management (Consultation approaches [e.g., referrals to specialists])

100. **Correct Answer:** A. Decreased sexual desire

**Rationale:** Decreased sexual desire, also known as low libido, is the MOST common indicator of sexual dysfunction. It can be influenced by various factors, including psychological, physical, and relational issues. While difficulty with arousal and inability to reach orgasm are also indicators of sexual dysfunction, decreased sexual desire is typically the most prevalent and can often lead to other sexual issues. Assessing for this indicator allows the social worker to explore potential underlying causes and address the client's concerns more comprehensively.

**Question Type:** Recall

**Content Area:** Assessment, Diagnosis, and Treatment Planning (The indicators of sexual dysfunction)

101. **Correct Answer:** C. Provide the client with the name and contact information of a referral

**Rationale:** When a client requests a referral to a specialist, the most appropriate action is to provide the client with the name and contact information of a referral. This respects the client's autonomy and preference for specialized care and ensures the client has the resources needed to pursue that care. Even though the social worker's supervisor believes in the social worker's competence, the client's request for a referral should be honored, especially if the client is seeking specialized support. Asking the supervisor to attend a session is not necessary if the supervisor has already confirmed the social worker's competence and the focus should be on facilitating the client's needs.

**Question Type:** Reasoning

**Content Area:** Psychotherapy, Clinical Interventions, and Case Management (Consultation approaches [e.g., referrals to specialists])

102. **Correct Answer:** B. Facilitate group problem-solving and communication

**Rationale:** While helping the team focus on common client goals and respecting the professional expertise of each team member are important aspects of collaboration, they are not sufficient on their own. Focusing on common goals is essential, but without effective communication and problem-solving, the team may struggle to achieve those goals. Respecting professional expertise is necessary, but it does not actively contribute to the collaboration process. The social worker must take an active role in facilitating group problem-solving and communication, ensuring that all voices are heard and that the team can work together efficiently to meet the client's needs. This approach promotes a cohesive and integrated care plan, leading to better outcomes for the client.

**Question Type:** Application

**Content Area:** Psychotherapy, Clinical Interventions, and Case Management (The process of interdisciplinary and intradisciplinary team collaboration)

103. **Correct Answer:** A. Reviewing staff job descriptions to identify the skills needed to deliver evidence-based interventions

**Rationale:** Reviewing staff job descriptions is MOST helpful as it allows the social worker to tailor the in-service training to the specific skills and competencies required for staff to effectively deliver evidence-based interventions. This ensures that the training is directly relevant to the staff's current roles and responsibilities, leading to better service delivery. Gathering information from professional colleagues about offerings that were valuable to their staff can provide useful insights but does not ensure that the training will be directly aligned with the specific needs and roles of the agency's staff. Determining licensure requirements for mandatory continuing education topics is important, but this focuses more on meeting regulatory requirements rather than on the specific skill development needed to enhance service delivery within the agency.

**Question Type:** Application

**Content Area:** Professional Values and Ethics (Professional development activities to improve practice and maintain current professional knowledge [e.g., in-service training, licensing requirements, reviews of literature, workshops])

104. **Correct Answer:** C. Ensure that all documentation is objective and relevant to the services provided

**Rationale:** Maintaining objective and relevant documentation is crucial for ethical and professional practice. This approach ensures that the records accurately reflect the services provided and the client's progress while adhering to ethical standards. Documentation should be clear and factual to support the integrity of the social worker's practice and provide a reliable account of the client's treatment, should it be required in legal contexts. Omitting sensitive information may lead to incomplete records and can be unethical as it fails to provide a complete account of the client's treatment and progress. Using vague language can compromise the quality and clarity of the documentation, potentially leading to misunderstandings and reducing the effectiveness of the records in supporting the client's treatment and care.

**Question Type:** Reasoning

**Content Area:** Professional Values and Ethics (Legal and/or ethical issues regarding documentation)

105. **Correct Answer:** C. Explore the client's past experiences with assertiveness

**Rationale:** When a client expresses discomfort with assertiveness, the social worker should NEXT understand the underlying reasons for this discomfort. By exploring the client's past experiences with assertiveness, the social worker can gain insights into any negative associations or fears that may be influencing the client's current attitude. This understanding is crucial before moving forward with strategies like practicing assertiveness or explaining concepts. This action allows the social worker to tailor the intervention to the client's specific needs and address any potential barriers effectively.

**Question Type:** Reasoning

**Content Area:** Psychotherapy, Clinical Interventions, and Case Management (Assertiveness training)

106. **Correct Answer:** C. Holding clients accountable for advancing cultural humility

**Rationale:** Social workers should demonstrate awareness and cultural humility by engaging in critical self-reflection (understanding their own bias and engaging in self-correction), recognizing clients as experts of their own culture, committing to lifelong learning, and holding *institutions* accountable for advancing cultural humility. The correct answer places the responsibility on clients, not institutions, for cultural humility which is not a requirement.

**Question Type:** Recall

**Content Area:** Human Development, Diversity, and Behavior in the Environment (The principles of culturally competent social work practice)

107. **Correct Answer:** B. Summary of the client's current treatment plan and progress toward goals

**Rationale:** The purpose of the case presentation in this context is to review the client's current situation and determine the best course of action. A summary of the client's current treatment plan and progress toward goals provides the multidisciplinary team with the most relevant information. This action allows the team to understand where the client is currently with regard to goal achievement and helps in generating informed recommendations for future interventions. Including a detailed history or potential interventions might be useful in other contexts but would not be the MOST helpful in guiding immediate decision-making.

**Question Type:** Reasoning

**Content Area:** Psychotherapy, Clinical Interventions, and Case Management (The elements of a case presentation)

108. **Correct Answer:** C. Protect the client's confidentiality when information is released or court ordered

**Rationale:** The request to keep psychotherapy notes separate from general medical records is MOST likely intended to safeguard client confidentiality. Psychotherapy notes, which contain more sensitive and detailed information, are kept separate to ensure they are not easily accessible to others or released in legal situations. This separation helps protect the client's privacy and ensures that sensitive therapeutic information remains confidential. While keeping notes separate does contribute to limited access, the primary reason for separating psychotherapy notes is to protect confidentiality, not just access control. Although psychotherapy notes can be more detailed, the main reason for keeping them separate is to maintain client confidentiality, especially in legal contexts. The Health Insurance Portability and Accountability Act (HIPAA) provides that psychotherapy notes are protected in a way that general health information is not. This means that while general medical records can be disclosed for treatment, payment, or healthcare operations without client consent, psychotherapy notes require explicit client authorization for disclosure, providing an extra layer of protection for the client's personal and sensitive information.

**Question Type:** Recall

**Content Area:** Professional Values and Ethics (Legal and/or ethical issues regarding documentation)

109. **Correct Answer:** B. Recent treatment plan

**Rationale:** When writing a session note, particularly with a client who has recently started a new treatment plan, the social worker must align the note with the objectives and strategies outlined in the most recent treatment plan. This document provides the current goals, interventions, and expected outcomes, ensuring that the session note accurately reflects the client's progress in relation to these factors. Consulting the intake assessment or prior session notes may provide background information but is not BEST for ensuring that the client's current treatment goals and progress are related to the recent treatment plan.

**Question Type:** Application

**Content Area:** Psychotherapy, Clinical Interventions, and Case Management (The principles of case recording, documentation, and management of practice records)

110. **Correct Answer:** A. Adhere to the agency's policy and conclude services

**Rationale:** The social worker must follow the agency's policy and conclude services as directed. Seeking external funding could be a viable option, but it may involve complex procedures and may not be authorized by the agency. There may be a reason why the agency limits services. For example, the agency may be licensed for only detoxification or emergency support. Providing services beyond the policy limit without informing the agency is unethical and could result in professional and legal consequences. Adhering to the policy ensures compliance with agency regulations, and providing referrals if needed remains the ethical course of action.

**Question Type:** Reasoning

**Content Area:** Professional Values and Ethics (Ethical issues in supervision and management)

111. **Correct Answer:** B. Racism is embedded in structures and woven into public policy.

**Rationale:** CRT posits that racism is not merely an individual issue but is embedded within societal structures and public policies. This perspective emphasizes that racial inequalities are systemic and institutionalized rather than just a matter of personal prejudices or biases. Therefore, CRT BEST focuses on understanding how racism is integrated into the fabric of societal institutions and practices, affecting outcomes across various aspects of life.

**Question Type:** Recall

**Content Area:** Human Development, Diversity, and Behavior in the Environment (Systemic [institutionalized] discrimination [e.g., racism, sexism, ageism])

112. **Correct Answer:** B. Offer counseling to address the family's emotional reactions to the diagnosis

**Rationale:** When a family is dealing with a recent diagnosis of Alzheimer's disease, addressing the emotional impact of the diagnosis FIRST is crucial. Offering counseling helps the family process their feelings, which can be overwhelming and distressing. This step is foundational before moving on to provide education or connect them with support groups. It ensures that the family is emotionally prepared to take in the information and utilize the resources available. While providing education about the progression of Alzheimer's disease and connecting the family with a support group are important, they are more effective after the family has had the opportunity to process their initial emotional reactions. Addressing the emotional response first helps to ensure that the family is in a better position to absorb information and seek additional support.

**Question Type:** Reasoning

**Content Area:** Assessment, Diagnosis, and Treatment Planning (Symptoms of neurologic and organic disorders)

113. **Correct Answer:** C. Current treatment plans

**Rationale:** When covering for a colleague, the most critical document for understanding how to manage a client's situation is the current treatment plan. This document outlines the client's active goals, interventions, and strategies, providing a roadmap for continuing the work without interruption. While recent treatment notes give context on recent sessions, the treatment plan offers a comprehensive view of what is supposed to be achieved and how to proceed. Intake assessments provide background information but may not reflect the client's current needs and objectives as effectively as the treatment plan does.

**Question Type:** Application

**Content Area:** Psychotherapy, Clinical Interventions, and Case Management (The principles of case recording, documentation, and management of practice records)

114. **Correct Answer:** C. Activities of daily living (ADLs)

**Rationale:** When evaluating an elderly person for nursing home care, the primary focus is often on ADLs. This is because ADLs are fundamental self-care tasks that are essential for basic personal functioning and survival. Nursing home care is typically considered when an individual is unable to perform these basic tasks independently, such as eating, bathing, dressing, toileting, transferring, and maintaining continence. ADLs provide a clear measure of the individual's ability to manage essential personal care activities. Difficulty with ADLs often indicates a significant level of impairment and a need for more intensive care and support, which is a primary consideration for nursing home placement. While IADLs and chronic medical conditions are also important factors in assessing overall needs and care planning, they are not as directly indicative of the need for nursing home care as issues with ADLs. IADLs reflect a person's ability to manage more complex aspects of daily life, such as finances and household management, which are important for community living but less critical for determining the necessity of nursing home care.

**Question Type:** Recall

**Content Area:** Human Development, Diversity, and Behavior in the Environment (The effect of disability on biopsychosocial functioning throughout the lifespan)

115. **Correct Answer:** C. Refer the client for a neurological evaluation to assess for possible underlying conditions

**Rationale:** The presence of memory lapses, coordination issues, and mood swings, especially when the client shows no concern, could indicate a serious neurological condition. The FIRST priority is to rule out any organic causes, such as neurodegenerative disorders or brain lesions, that might be contributing to these symptoms. A neurological evaluation is critical in identifying any underlying conditions that require immediate medical intervention. While cognitive behavioral therapy might address the symptoms if they were purely psychological, it is essential to first determine whether there is an underlying neurological condition. Exploring stressors might provide context, but it does not address the potential for a medical issue that could explain the sudden onset of these symptoms.

**Question Type:** Reasoning

**Content Area:** Assessment, Diagnosis, and Treatment Planning (Symptoms of neurologic and organic disorders)

116. **Correct Answer:** B. Ask the client about how cultural and spiritual practices impact overall well-being

**Rationale:** A shaman is a practitioner who uses spiritual rituals, divination, and other traditional methods to provide healing and guidance, often drawing on cultural and spiritual beliefs. When a client integrates such practices into coping strategies, it is BEST for the social worker to understand how these practices impact the client's mental health and overall well-being. This approach respects the client's cultural and spiritual beliefs while ensuring that these practices are considered in the context of therapeutic needs. Simply determining the source of distress or recommending continued sessions with the shaman without exploring the impact may overlook the importance of integrating the client's cultural and spiritual practices into a comprehensive treatment plan.

**Question Type:** Reasoning

**Content Area:** Human Development, Diversity, and Behavior in the Environment (The effect of culture, race, and ethnicity on behaviors, attitudes, and identity)

117. **Correct Answer:** B. Improve coordination of services to avoid duplication

**Rationale:** When crafting an affiliation agreement between two service providers, the primary goal is MOST often to improve the coordination of services and avoid duplication. By establishing clear roles and responsibilities through the agreement, the social worker helps ensure that the services provided by each organization complement each other rather than overlap, which enhances the overall effectiveness of the service network for individuals struggling with housing stability. While establishing services and shared responsibility are important, improving coordination and avoiding duplication directly addresses the efficiency and integration of the service network.

**Question Type:** Application

**Content Area:** Psychotherapy, Clinical Interventions, and Case Management (Methods to establish service networks or community resources)

118. **Correct Answer:** A. Seek supervision to discuss the impact of the burnout

**Rationale:** Seeking supervision allows the social worker to address concerns about burnout and its effects on professional practice specifically and generally. This approach provides an opportunity to explore strategies for managing workload and self-care with guidance from a supervisor. While advocating for self-care programs is valuable, it does not address the immediate need for support and solutions. This response choice is also not focused on the impacts on client care, which need to be paramount. Requesting a workload reduction does not address underlying systemic issues as other social workers may be experiencing similar problems.

Reducing the responsibilities of one worker does not positively come up with a solution for all.

**Question Type:** Reasoning

**Content Area:** Professional Values and Ethics (Social worker self-care principles and techniques)

**119. Correct Answer:** B. Work with the client to maintain cultural practices within new social structures and norms

**Rationale:** Acculturation refers to the process of adapting to a new culture while retaining elements of one's original cultural identity. For a client who has immigrated from another country due to political conflict, supporting the client in maintaining cultural practices within new social structures and norms is BEST. This approach helps the client preserve the client's cultural heritage, which can provide emotional support and a sense of continuity during the transition. It also assists in adapting to the new environment in a way that respects the client's background. While engaging in community activities and understanding social structures are important, maintaining cultural practices ensures that the client's identity is preserved and integrated into a new environment, fostering a smoother and more respectful acculturation process.

**Question Type:** Reasoning

**Content Area:** Human Development, Diversity, and Behavior in the Environment (The impact of globalization on clients/client systems [e.g., interrelatedness of systems, international integration, technology, environmental or financial crises, epidemics])

**120. Correct Answer:** C. The social worker wants to understand the client's feelings about this recent change in health status.

**Rationale:** During the assessment phase, the social worker is MOST likely focused on gathering information to understand the client's current situation and emotional state. Subjective data, such as the client's feelings and perceptions, are essential for gaining insight into how the client is coping with the recent health change. While processing the experience and its impact on the client's quality of life is crucial, it typically occurs during the intervention phase rather than the assessment phase. The focus on understanding feelings is a key part of building rapport and forming a foundation for future interventions. There is no indication in the question that the client does not understand the protocols associated with treatment.

**Question Type:** Reasoning

**Content Area:** Assessment, Diagnosis, and Treatment Planning (The principles and features of objective and subjective data)

121. **Correct Answer:** C. Segregation of poor individuals into low-income areas within communities

**Rationale:** Social stratification involves the hierarchical arrangement of individuals in society based on factors such as socioeconomic status, which leads to unequal access to resources and opportunities. Social segregation occurs when poor individuals are segregated into low-income areas, which often results in limited access to quality education, healthcare, and other resources, reflecting systemic inequalities. The affinity for those to socialize within their own socioeconomic status describes a social tendency rather than stratification, and receiving more opportunities due to social status addresses individual advantages rather than systemic social hierarchies.

**Question Type:** Application

**Content Area:** Human Development, Diversity, and Behavior in the Environment (Systemic [institutionalized] discrimination [e.g., racism, sexism, ageism])

122. **Correct Answer:** C. Boards of directors

**Rationale:** The board of directors is primarily responsible for formally setting the strategic direction of a social service organization. They provide oversight and make high-level decisions that guide the organization's mission, vision, and long-term goals. While the executive director and agency administrators play crucial roles in implementing the strategies and managing day-to-day operations, the board of directors is responsible for setting the overarching strategic priorities and direction for an organization.

**Question Type:** Recall

**Content Area:** Psychotherapy, Clinical Interventions, and Case Management (Governance structures)

123. **Correct Answer:** A. Implement a performance-based funding system

**Rationale:** Implementing a performance-based funding system can BEST address the inability of a service organization to meet its goals by linking funding to the achievement of specific outcomes. This approach can incentivize staff to focus on achieving goals and ensure that resources are allocated effectively based on performance. By tying financial support to measurable results, the organization can better align resources with its strategic objectives and improve overall effectiveness. While determining daily resource needs is important for understanding immediate gaps, a performance-based funding system addresses the root cause by driving performance and optimizing resource allocation. Engaging in fundraising can also be beneficial but does not directly address performance issues.

**Question Type:** Recall

**Content Area:** Psychotherapy, Clinical Interventions, and Case Management (Methods to establish program objectives and outcomes)

124. **Correct Answer:** A. Advocate that clients are not required to disclose traumatic experiences during intake

**Rationale:** Trauma-informed care principles emphasize creating a safe and supportive environment for clients. This includes respecting autonomy and not forcing disclosure of traumatic experiences if not ready. While training staff on sensitivity and gathering client feedback are important, allowing clients to choose what they disclose during intake directly addresses their distress and aligns with trauma-informed care practices.

**Question Type:** Reasoning

**Content Area:** Assessment, Diagnosis, and Treatment Planning (Theories of trauma-informed care)

125. **Correct Answer:** B. Experimental design

**Rationale:** This study is an experimental design because it includes the key elements of random assignment of clients into two groups (new CBT program vs. standard treatment) and the measurement of outcomes before and after the intervention. Experimental designs are used to establish cause-and-effect relationships by controlling for confounding variables and providing a high level of internal validity.

**Question Type:** Application

**Content Area:** Assessment, Diagnosis, and Treatment Planning (Basic and applied research design and methods)

126. **Correct Answer:** A. Conduct a structured assessment of the supervisees' skills and knowledge gaps

**Rationale:** To MOST effectively identify the learning needs of supervisees and develop targeted learning objectives, the social work supervisor should conduct a structured assessment of the supervisees' skills and knowledge gaps. This approach provides a systematic and objective evaluation of specific areas where supervisees require additional support, ensuring that learning objectives are well informed and relevant to their developmental needs. Observing supervisees during their work can offer valuable insights into their practical skills and performance but may not fully capture all learning needs or knowledge gaps. Observations might focus on specific tasks or behaviors, potentially overlooking broader skill deficits and underlying issues. Additionally, this method can be subjective and lacks the comprehensive analysis needed to address specific learning needs effectively. Asking supervisees about their career goals and interests helps understand their aspirations and motivations, but this approach may not directly reveal their current learning needs or knowledge gaps. Supervisees' career goals might not align with their immediate developmental needs, and their interests might not highlight critical areas requiring support. This method provides useful context but lacks the structured, objective evaluation necessary for developing precise and targeted learning objectives.

**Question Type:** Reasoning

**Content Area:** Psychotherapy, Clinical Interventions, and Case Management (Methods to identify learning needs and develop learning objectives for supervisees)

127. **Correct Answer:** A. Conducting a survey to gather feedback from staff members on their experiences with internal communication

**Rationale:** Conducting a survey to gather feedback from staff members is the MOST effective way to collect relevant data on communication patterns within the organization. This method allows the social worker to understand how communication is experienced and perceived by those directly involved, providing valuable insights into the effectiveness and challenges of internal communication. Reviewing organizational documents would help understand formal communication structures but may not capture how communication is actually practiced. Reading agency newsletters and internal memos can give some insight into the organization's communication style and transparency but lacks the direct feedback needed to assess overall communication patterns.

**Question Type:** Reasoning

**Content Area:** Assessment, Diagnosis, and Treatment Planning (Methods to assess organizational functioning [e.g., agency assessments])

128. **Correct Answer:** B. Regression analysis

**Rationale:** Regression analysis is the MOST appropriate method for examining whether there are disparities in dropout rates based on demographic factors. This statistical technique allows the social worker to assess the relationship between independent variables (such as age, race, or income) and the dependent variable (dropout rates). By using regression analysis, the social worker can determine if certain demographic characteristics are statistically significant predictors of dropout rates and the strength of these relationships. Descriptive statistics would only summarize the data, such as calculating averages or percentages, without identifying relationships between variables. Content analysis, on the other hand, is used for analyzing qualitative data, such as text or interview transcripts, and would not be suitable for examining patterns in a large quantitative data set. Therefore, regression analysis is the best method to explore and quantify the impact of demographic factors on dropout rates in this scenario.

**Question Type:** Application

**Content Area:** Assessment, Diagnosis, and Treatment Planning (Data collection and analysis methods)

129. **Correct Answer:** A. Summative evaluation

**Rationale:** A summative evaluation is MOST helpful when deciding whether to replicate a program because it assesses the overall effectiveness and outcomes of the program after its implementation. This type of evaluation provides a comprehensive analysis of whether the program achieved its intended goals, the impact it had on participants, and the overall success of the initiative. By examining the results and effectiveness of the program, the administrator can make an informed decision about whether it is worth replicating. Formative evaluation, while useful for improving a program during its development and early implementation stages, is not designed to provide a final assessment of the program's success, which is crucial for deciding on replication. Cost-benefit evaluation focuses on analyzing the financial costs versus the benefits of a program, which is important for understanding the economic efficiency of a program but does not provide a comprehensive assessment of its overall effectiveness and impact in the way a summative evaluation does.

**Question Type:** Application

**Content Area:** Psychotherapy, Clinical Interventions, and Case Management (The effects of program evaluation findings on services)

**130. Correct Answer:** A. Test–retest

**Rationale:** The test–retest method is used to assess the reliability of a measurement tool by administering the same test to the same group of individuals at two different points in time. The social worker is using this method to ensure that the results are consistent over time, indicating the reliability of the measurement tools. Interrater reliability involves comparing the results of different evaluators, while internal consistency assesses the consistency of results across items within a single test, making them less relevant to the scenario described.

**Question Type:** Application

**Content Area:** Assessment, Diagnosis, and Treatment Planning (Methods to assess reliability and validity in social work research)

**131. Correct Answer:** A. Content validity

**Rationale:** Content validity is MOST at risk in this scenario because the risk assessment tool is missing important factors that are relevant to accurately assessing the likelihood of reoffending. Content validity refers to how well a measurement tool covers the entire range of the concept it is supposed to measure. If critical factors are omitted, the tool may not fully or accurately measure the risk, thereby compromising its content validity. Criterion-related validity refers to how well one measure predicts an outcome based on another measure. It is often assessed by comparing the tool in question to a known standard or outcome. Construct validity, on the other hand, is the extent to which a test or instrument measures the theoretical construct or concept it is intended to measure. While both criterion-related and construct validity are important, they are less directly impacted by missing content than content validity.

**Question Type:** Application

**Content Area:** Assessment, Diagnosis, and Treatment Planning (Methods to assess reliability and validity in social work research)

**132. Correct Answer:** B. Development of social skills and focus on academic and extracurricular activities

**Rationale:** The latency stage, occurring between ages 5 and puberty, is BEST characterized by a period where sexual desires become less prominent. Instead, children focus on developing social skills, engaging in academic pursuits, and participating in extracurricular activities. This stage emphasizes the development of competencies and building peer relationships. Moving away from the focus on sexual desires and toward forming emotional relationships usually occurs in adulthood. Exploration of sexual identity formation is more relevant to earlier stages like the phallic stage, where children first experience the development of sexual identity.

**Question Type:** Recall

**Content Area:** Psychotherapy, Clinical Interventions, and Case Management (Psychoanalytic and psychodynamic approaches)

133. **Correct Answer:** B. Encourage collaborative decision-making

**Rationale:** Encouraging collaborative decision-making is the MOST effective approach to improving team cohesion and productivity in this scenario. By involving team members in the decision-making process, the social work manager fosters a sense of ownership and shared responsibility among the team. This approach helps to build trust, increase engagement, and ensure that all members feel valued and heard, which can lead to improved morale and more consistent performance. Asking team members to engage in cooperative performance monitoring focuses on performance monitoring, which, while useful, might not directly address underlying issues related to team cohesion or morale. Monitoring can sometimes feel punitive if not implemented carefully, potentially exacerbating morale issues. Delegating tasks to team members based on their strengths is also important for effective team management, as it ensures that tasks are aligned with individual competencies. However, without addressing the need for collaborative input and shared decision-making, this approach alone may not fully resolve issues related to team cohesion and overall morale.

**Question Type:** Application

**Content Area:** Psychotherapy, Clinical Interventions, and Case Management (Leadership and management techniques)

134. **Correct Answer:** C. Direct the conversation to the substance use for further exploration

**Rationale:** The social worker is MOST likely confronting the client about the substance use to direct the conversation toward this issue for further exploration. Confrontation in a therapeutic context is often used to bring attention to something that the client may be avoiding or minimizing. By doing so, the social worker can guide the client to engage more deeply with the topic, which is essential for understanding the underlying issues and addressing them effectively. Helping the client to see that the usage is a problem is a possible outcome of confrontation, but the primary goal of the confrontation technique itself is to focus the conversation on the area that requires attention. Demonstrating that the social worker does not condone the denial is not the primary reason for using confrontation, as the technique is more about facilitating the client's self-exploration rather than expressing the social worker's personal stance.

**Question Type:** Reasoning

**Content Area:** Psychotherapy, Clinical Interventions, and Case Management (The principles and techniques of interviewing [e.g., supporting, clarifying, focusing, confronting, validating, feedback, reflecting, language differences, use of interpreters, redirecting])

135. **Correct Answer:** C. Social workers provide all necessary information in a way that clients can easily understand.

**Rationale:** Social workers must communicate in a manner that is clear and accessible to clients, enabling them to make informed decisions. Social workers can provide information in an accessible format but cannot guarantee that clients understand this information. While it is crucial for clients to understand the risks and benefits of proposed interventions, the MOST important focus of informed consent is not just on conveying specific details like risks and benefits but on ensuring that clients fully understand all aspects of the intervention. The correct answer emphasizes clear and understandable communication, which is in the control of social workers and, therefore, the most comprehensive and ethically sound approach.

**Question Type:** Reasoning

**Content Area:** Professional Values and Ethics (The principles and processes of obtaining informed consent)

136. **Correct Answer:** B. "Please share what you think might be triggering these intense feelings at work."

**Rationale:** After reflecting on the client's maladaptive feelings, the NEXT step in the problem-solving process is to explore the underlying causes of those feelings. Asking the client to share what the client thinks might be triggering the intense emotions helps to delve deeper into the root causes of the stress. This exploration is crucial for understanding the specific factors contributing to the client's distress and for developing effective strategies to address those issues. Telling a client that feelings are understandable is a validation statement, which is important but comes before exploring the underlying causes. It does not move the conversation forward in terms of problem-solving. Reviewing what has been talked about is a useful summary and planning statement but typically occurs later in the session, after the exploration of underlying issues. It focuses on summarizing and planning rather than delving into the causes of the current emotional state.

**Question Type:** Reasoning

**Content Area:** Psychotherapy, Clinical Interventions, and Case Management (The principles and techniques of interviewing [e.g., supporting, clarifying, focusing, confronting, validating, feedback, reflecting, language differences, use of interpreters, redirecting])

137. **Correct Answer:** B. Reviewing the records to refresh the social worker's memory of the client's history and progress

**Rationale:** Reviewing client records to refresh the social worker's memory is the MOST appropriate use of client records because it directly supports effective service delivery while respecting client confidentiality. This action ensures that the social worker remains informed about the client's history, treatment progress, and current needs, which is essential for providing quality care. Confidentiality is a core principle in social work, and client records should only be shared with colleagues if there is a clear, justifiable reason, and usually with the client's informed consent. Simply seeking advice on treatment options does not automatically justify sharing sensitive client information unless specific protocols are followed. While educating others in the agency is important, this option is incorrect because using actual client records for training purposes can violate client confidentiality. Even if identifying information is removed, there is still a risk of breaching confidentiality, especially if those being trained could potentially identify the client.

**Question Type:** Recall

**Content Area:** Professional Values and Ethics (The use of client/client system records)

138. **Correct Answer:** C. Differentiate the self by helping individuals establish healthier boundaries

**Rationale:** Bowenian therapy, also known as Bowen family systems therapy, focuses on helping individuals within a family achieve differentiation. Differentiation is the process of developing a strong sense of self while maintaining emotional connections with others. This approach emphasizes managing emotional reactivity and establishing healthy boundaries, which allows individuals to function more independently within their family systems. While emotional closeness is valued, Bowenian therapy does not aim to increase interdependence. Instead, it seeks to balance connection with individuality. Improving communication patterns is not the primary focus of Bowenian therapy, even though it might be addressed during the therapeutic process. The PRIMARY goal is to enhance differentiation and self-regulation. Bowenian therapy is aimed at helping individuals differentiate themselves, manage their emotional responses, and create healthier boundaries within the family dynamic.

**Question Type:** Recall

**Content Area:** Psychotherapy, Clinical Interventions, and Case Management (Family therapy models, interventions, and approaches)

139. **Correct Answer:** A. Review case records to ensure that documentation meets agency and regulatory standards

**Rationale:** As part of a quality assurance initiative, a social worker should focus on activities that help monitor and improve the quality of services provided. Reviewing case records to ensure that documentation meets agency and regulatory standards is a key aspect of quality assurance. This process helps ensure that the agency is compliant with legal and ethical standards, which is essential for improving service delivery and client outcomes. Increasing client engagement by asking clients about enhanced supports needed is focused on direct client service rather than on quality assurance. While client feedback is important, quality assurance primarily involves assessing and improving internal processes and documentation. Advocating for additional staff training on best practice interventions is an important part of professional development but is not the primary focus of quality assurance. Quality assurance is more about evaluating current practices and ensuring they meet required standards.

**Question Type:** Reasoning

**Content Area:** Psychotherapy, Clinical Interventions, and Case Management (Quality assurance, including program reviews and audits by external sources)

140. **Correct Answer:** A. Ability to perform daily activities

**Rationale:** The client's ability to perform daily activities is the MOST crucial factor in deciding whether the client can safely return home or require further rehabilitation. While the client's desire to return home and long-term prognosis are important considerations, the primary focus will be on ensuring that the client can independently manage daily needs and maintain safety outside of a structured care environment.

**Question Type:** Application

**Content Area:** Assessment, Diagnosis, and Treatment Planning (Placement options based on assessed level of care)

141. **Correct Answer:** C. "Could you describe more about the specific changes in your job role that are making you feel unsupported?"

**Rationale:** Asking the client about the changes that result in feeling unsupported is the BEST choice because it encourages the client to articulate the specific aspects of the situation that are contributing to feelings of anxiety and being overwhelmed. This approach is supportive as it demonstrates a willingness to understand the client's unique experience and challenges. The correct answer allows the client to explore and discuss the root causes of the distress, which is essential for developing targeted interventions and strategies to address the concerns. Acknowledging feeling overwhelmed and encouraging discussion about it is supportive but focuses more on offering solutions and managing anxiety rather than first understanding the specific issues causing the client's feelings. Normalizing the feelings and telling the client to stay positive may be well intentioned but can come across as dismissive of the client's current feelings. It emphasizes general resilience rather than addressing the specific concerns and emotions the client is experiencing. The correct answer is best as it directly addresses the client's immediate need to discuss and explore the factors contributing to the feelings, thereby providing a foundation for meaningful support.

**Question Type:** Reasoning

**Content Area:** Psychotherapy, Clinical Interventions, and Case Management (The principles and techniques of interviewing [e.g., supporting, clarifying, focusing, confronting, validating, feedback, reflecting, language differences, use of interpreters, redirecting])

142. **Correct Answer:** B. Report the issue to the appropriate authorities after discussing the situation with the client

**Rationale:** Ethically, social workers must uphold honesty and integrity in all professional activities. Supporting the client in providing false information would be a breach of ethical standards and could have legal repercussions. The social worker should first discuss the situation with the client, explaining the seriousness of falsifying information. Then, the social worker must report the issue to the appropriate authorities to address the misrepresentation properly. This approach ensures adherence to ethical and legal standards while addressing the client's actions transparently.

Advising the client of the risks associated with continuing to provide false information is not the most appropriate response because it does not fully address the ethical and legal responsibilities of the social worker. While advising the client about the risks is important, it does not resolve the issue of falsification or protect the integrity of the process.

**Question Type:** Reasoning

**Content Area:** Professional Values and Ethics (Legal and/or ethical issues related to the practice of social work, including responsibility to clients/client systems, colleagues, the profession, and society)

**143. Correct Answer:** A. Chaining

**Rationale:** Chaining is the technique used in this scenario. The social worker breaks down the complex task of using the bathroom into smaller, manageable steps (e.g., locking the door, washing hands, using toilet paper) and then helps the student to master each step independently. Once each step is learned, the social worker sequences these steps into a complete routine, aiming for the student to perform the entire sequence of behaviors independently. Shaping involves reinforcing successive approximations toward a desired behavior. While shaping focuses on gradually improving performance by reinforcing closer approximations to the final goal, chaining is MOST likely being used as the scenario describes linking discrete steps together to form a complete behavior. Modeling involves demonstrating a behavior for the client to observe and imitate. In this scenario, the focus is on breaking down and sequencing behaviors rather than demonstrating them for imitation, so modeling is not the primary technique used here.

**Question Type:** Application

**Content Area:** Psychotherapy, Clinical Interventions, and Case Management (Cognitive and behavioral interventions)

**144. Correct Answer:** A. Being distressed by compulsive handwashing despite knowing it is excessive

**Rationale:** Ego-dystonic behavior refers to actions or thoughts that are in conflict with the individual's self-image or values and cause significant distress. In the correct answer, the client is experiencing distress about the compulsive handwashing, which is recognized as excessive, reflecting a clear mismatch between the behavior and self-perception. Consistently arriving late describes a behavior that may be problematic but does not necessarily involve internal conflict or distress about the behavior itself. Suffering from depressive episodes, while describing a serious issue, pertains more to emotional distress and depression rather than the specific concept of ego-dystonic behavior.

**Question Type:** Recall

**Content Area:** Psychotherapy, Clinical Interventions, and Case Management (Psychoanalytic and psychodynamic approaches)

**145. Correct Answer:** B. Assess whether the client has taken any actions to modify negative behaviors

**Rationale:** To MOST effectively assess a client's motivation to change, evaluating actions toward modifying negative behaviors provides direct evidence of the client's readiness and commitment. This approach looks beyond mere intentions or understandings and focuses on tangible steps the client has already taken. Actions reflect a client's engagement and effort, which are most crucial for gauging readiness for change. The incorrect response choices focus more on understanding consequences and self-belief rather than the actual steps taken toward change.

**Question Type:** Reasoning

**Content Area:** Assessment, Diagnosis, and Treatment Planning (The indicators of motivation, resistance, and readiness to change)

**146. Correct Answer:** B. Coordinating services and support to help the client manage the illness

**Rationale:** The correct answer is the BEST approach, encompassing the role of providing clinical counseling and medication management as well as promoting independence and role fulfillment. Such an answer is often referred to as "an umbrella option." By coordinating services and support, the social worker addresses the client's needs from a holistic perspective, including physical, emotional, and social environments. This approach aligns with the person-in-environment (PIE) perspective, which considers how various external and internal factors impact the client's well-being and functioning. Social work differs from psychology which focuses on treating the illness. Promoting independence and role fulfillment is important, but there are other aspects of social work care that are not covered by this response choice.

**Question Type:** Recall

**Content Area:** Human Development, Diversity, and Behavior in the Environment (Person-in-environment [PIE] theory)

147. **Correct Answer:** C. Assess the client's current functioning

**Rationale:** A mental status examination (MSE) is MOST often used to evaluate a client's current cognitive and emotional functioning. This includes assessing aspects such as mood, orientation, thought processes, and insight, which are critical for understanding the client's present state and planning appropriate interventions. One incorrect response choice focuses on long-term therapy engagement, which is not the primary goal of an MSE. Another incorrect response choice, while important, is more specific to assessing immediate safety rather than overall functioning.

**Question Type:** Reasoning

**Content Area:** Assessment, Diagnosis, and Treatment Planning (The components and function of the mental status examination)

148. **Correct Answer:** C. Current assaultive behavior

**Rationale:** The MOST helpful factor in determining whether a client should be evaluated for involuntary commitment is current assaultive behavior. This indicates an immediate risk of harm to the client or others, which is the primary criterion for involuntary commitment. While prior incidents of self-harm or violence and inability to make progress in treatment are important considerations, they are less critical than current behaviors that pose an imminent threat.

**Question Type:** Application

**Content Area:** Assessment, Diagnosis, and Treatment Planning (The indicators and risk factors of the client's/client system's danger to self and others)

149. **Correct Answer:** B. Open-ended assessment

**Rationale:** When gathering sensitive information, especially related to past trauma, an open-ended assessment is the MOST effective method. This approach allows the student to share experiences in a nonthreatening, flexible environment where they can guide the conversation. It helps to build trust and rapport, making the student more comfortable discussing difficult topics. In contrast, structured interviews and written surveys might feel too rigid or impersonal, potentially leading to less disclosure or discomfort for the student.

**Question Type:** Recall

**Content Area:** Assessment, Diagnosis, and Treatment Planning (Methods to obtain sensitive information [e.g., substance abuse, sexual abuse])

150. **Correct Answer:** B. Develop a relapse prevention plan with the client

**Rationale:** Developing a relapse prevention plan with the client is the FIRST step because it addresses the comprehensive needs of maintaining sobriety. This plan includes identifying strategies for managing stress and preventing relapse ("an umbrella option"), which naturally incorporates connecting the client with support groups and resources. While understanding the client's triggers and history is important, the relapse prevention plan provides a structured approach to addressing both immediate and ongoing recovery needs. The correct answer is a planning task which also precedes connecting to a resource, which is an intervention. Having the social worker learn more about the client's history and triggers does not directly help with sustained recovery.

**Question Type:** Reasoning

**Content Area:** Human Development, Diversity, and Behavior in the Environment (Addiction theories and concepts)

151. **Correct Answer:** C. Facilitate a community discussion to develop a common identification of the concerns

**Rationale:** Utilizing a social constructivism approach, which emphasizes that social realities are created through interactions and shared meanings, the social worker should facilitate a community discussion to develop a common identification of the concerns. This approach helps build a shared understanding among community members by collaboratively defining and addressing the issues, fostering a unified perspective that can drive effective social change. This method contrasts with simply leveraging existing power structures or relying solely on leaders to define issues, as it engages community members in constructing their own collective reality and solutions.

**Question Type:** Reasoning

**Content Area:** Human Development, Diversity, and Behavior in the Environment (Theories of social change and community development)

152. **Correct Answer:** A. Use a standardized trauma assessment tool to screen the client for trauma

**Rationale:** When a social worker suspects that a client has experienced significant trauma, the FIRST step is to use a standardized trauma assessment tool. These tools are specifically designed to identify the presence and extent of trauma-related symptoms and experiences, providing a structured and reliable way to screen for trauma. Many social workers rely on the Adverse Childhood Experiences (ACE) Questionnaire. The ACE Questionnaire includes 10 items that ask about various forms of abuse, neglect, and household dysfunction, such as parental substance abuse or divorce. Exploring coping mechanisms and conducting a biopsychosocial assessment are also important, but they are more effective after confirming the presence of trauma through an initial screening.

**Question Type:** Recall

**Content Area:** Assessment, Diagnosis, and Treatment Planning (Methods used to assess trauma)

153. **Correct Answer:** A. Negative feedback and criticism from significant others

**Rationale:** Negative feedback and criticism from significant others can impact a person's self-image. These interactions often contribute to negative self-perceptions and can have a profound effect on how individuals view themselves. While personal achievements and societal trends are also relevant, the immediate impact of critical feedback from close relationships tends to be more direct and influential in shaping a client's self-image. Just because a client is aware of societal trends and media portrayals does not mean that the client is impacted by them.

**Question Type:** Reasoning

**Content Area:** Human Development, Diversity, and Behavior in the Environment (Factors influencing self-image [e.g., culture, race, religion/ spirituality, age, disability, trauma])

154. **Correct Answer:** A. Identify the student's specific learning strengths and weaknesses

**Rationale:** Identifying the student's specific learning strengths and weaknesses helps the social worker to understand the student's unique learning profile. By identifying specific strengths and weaknesses, the social worker can MOST effectively develop tailored interventions to address the student's academic struggles, which are likely contributing to frustration and low self-esteem. While comparing the student's performance with peers can provide context, it does not directly address the individual needs of the student. Similarly, diagnosing a learning disability is a more specific outcome that may or may not be relevant depending on the test results, but the immediate goal is to assess how the student learns best and where they may need additional support to address the frustration and self-esteem which are explicitly mentioned in the question.

**Question Type:** Application

**Content Area:** Assessment, Diagnosis, and Treatment Planning (Methods to incorporate the results of psychological and educational tests into assessment)

155. **Correct Answer:** B. Appearing disheveled and having bloodshot eyes with dilated pupils

**Rationale:** Physical signs of appearing disheveled, bloodshot eyes, and dilated pupils are MOST commonly associated with drug misuse. These observable symptoms are often direct indicators of substance use, whereas trouble at work, isolation, and changes in sleep patterns and appetite, while potentially related to drug misuse, are more general and can also be influenced by other factors. Physical signs are the most reliable as they can be easily observed but are not always evident as they are in this scenario.

**Question Type:** Application

**Content Area:** Human Development, Diversity, and Behavior in the Environment (The effects of addiction and substance abuse on individuals, families, groups, organizations, and communities)

156. **Correct Answer:** C. Dependent personality disorder

**Rationale:** Dependent personality disorder is BEST characterized by an excessive need to be taken care of, leading to submissive and clinging behavior and fears of separation. The client's difficulty making decisions without reassurance, fear of not managing independently, and tolerance of mistreatment to avoid abandonment are hallmark traits of this disorder. While borderline personality disorder also involves fear of abandonment, it typically includes more intense emotional instability and impulsive behaviors. Avoidant personality disorder involves fears of rejection and social inhibition but not necessarily a dependency on others to the same extent seen in dependent personality disorder.

**Question Type:** Application

**Content Area:** Assessment, Diagnosis, and Treatment Planning (The use of the Diagnostic and Statistical Manual of the American Psychiatric Association)

157. **Correct Answer:** B. Monoamine oxidase inhibitor (MAOI)

**Rationale:** MAOIs are a type of antidepressant that can interact dangerously with foods high in tyramine, such as aged cheeses and cured meats. This interaction can lead to a hypertensive crisis, which is why clients taking MAOIs must follow strict dietary restrictions. While SSRIs and TCAs are also used to treat depression, they do not require such dietary precautions, making MAOIs the MOST likely medication the client is taking.

**Question Type:** Application

**Content Area:** Assessment, Diagnosis, and Treatment Planning (Common psychotropic and non-psychotropic prescriptions and over-the-counter medications and their side effects)

158. **Correct Answer:** C. Discuss the client's financial difficulties with a supervisor to explore potential options

**Rationale:** The social worker should address the client's financial difficulties while respecting agency policies and ethical guidelines. Discussing the situation with a supervisor allows the social worker to explore potential solutions, such as the possibility of using the scholarship fund, without breaching confidentiality or agency rules. This approach ensures that the client's needs are considered and that any support provided is done in an ethical and policy-compliant manner. Disclosing the fund against agency policy could have negative consequences for the social worker which ultimately does not help the client. Solely focusing on alternative treatments may be unnecessary if the social worker can access the scholarship funds for the client to continuing therapy.

**Question Type:** Reasoning

**Content Area:** Professional Values and Ethics (Legal and/or ethical issues related to the practice of social work, including responsibility to clients/client systems, colleagues, the profession, and society)

159. **Correct Answer:** B. Data triangulation

**Rationale:** Data triangulation involves using multiple sources of information to gain a comprehensive and reliable understanding of a client's issues. By combining clinical interviews, client self-reports, and input from family members, the social worker is employing data triangulation to validate and enrich the assessment process. This approach helps to cross-check and corroborate findings, reducing bias and increasing the accuracy of the assessment. A systematic review is a method used to comprehensively gather and analyze existing research on a particular topic. It is not specific to individual client assessments and does not involve using multiple sources of information from within the context of a single case. A needs assessment is a process used to determine the needs or gaps within a population or community. It is focused on identifying and prioritizing the needs of a larger group rather than assessing an individual client's issues through multiple sources of information.

**Question Type:** Application

**Content Area:** Assessment, Diagnosis, and Treatment Planning (The factors and processes used in problem formulation)

160. **Correct Answer:** B. Reduce the negative effects of unsupported reentry leading to recidivism

**Rationale:** The expansion of social workers in public defender offices is primarily driven by the 2010 Supreme Court ruling in *Padilla v. Kentucky*. This case emphasized that public defenders need to consider the collateral consequences of criminal justice involvement, such as immigration status, housing, and eligibility for government assistance programs. These factors can contribute to unsupported reentry, which often leads to future recidivism. By incorporating social workers, public defender offices aim to address these issues comprehensively and support clients' successful reintegration into society.

**Question Type:** Recall

**Content Area:** Human Development, Diversity, and Behavior in the Environment (Criminal justice systems)

161. **Correct Answer:** A. Policies and institutions that define criminal activity and punish those engaging in such activity

**Rationale:** The carceral system encompasses the network of policies, institutions, and practices designed to manage and penalize individuals convicted of crimes. This definition BEST captures the core function of the carceral system, which is to define criminal behavior and implement punishment for those who engage in such behavior. It focuses on the system's role in managing and enforcing legal consequences, distinguishing it from preventive measures or support services.

**Question Type:** Recall

**Content Area:** Human Development, Diversity, and Behavior in the Environment (Criminal justice systems)

162. **Correct Answer:** A. Genogram

**Rationale:** A genogram is a graphic tool used to map out family relationships, including patterns and connections across generations. This is particularly useful in visualizing complex family backgrounds and intergenerational trauma. An ecomap, in contrast, is used to illustrate the client's relationships with the external environment, including community resources, rather than family relationships. A client self-report involves gathering information directly from the client, but it does not provide a visual representation of family dynamics, which is the key feature of a genogram. Additionally, a client self-report aims to gather client's personal perspectives on feelings, behaviors, and experiences which are not mentioned in the question, though they may be valuable in assessment.

**Question Type:** Application

**Content Area:** Assessment, Diagnosis, and Treatment Planning (Techniques and instruments used to assess clients/client systems)

**163. Correct Answer:** B. Decline the request to maintain professional boundaries

**Rationale:** It is essential for social workers to maintain professional boundaries with clients, even after the therapeutic relationship has ended. Accepting a social media connection could blur these boundaries, potentially compromising confidentiality and the professional nature of the relationship. By declining the request, the social worker upholds ethical standards and reinforces the importance of maintaining clear, professional relationships. Ignoring the request could be perceived as dismissive and does not provide the former client with an understanding of why the request cannot be accepted, while accepting the request could lead to ethical and professional complications.

**Question Type:** Reasoning

**Content Area:** Professional Values and Ethics (Professional boundaries in the social worker-client/client system relationship [e.g., power differences, conflicts of interest, etc.])

**164. Correct Answer:** B. Restore the family's daily routines and emotional state to before crisis levels

**Rationale:** In this scenario, the primary goal is to help the family regain stability and return to their precrisis state. Therefore, restoring the family's daily routines and emotional state to before crisis levels is most appropriate. While building resilience to strengthen the family's ability to handle future stressors is valuable for long-term coping, it does not address the immediate need to stabilize the family in the wake of the current crisis. Exploring the impact of these events on communication and relationship patterns is also important but serves a more diagnostic purpose rather than providing immediate support and stabilization. Thus, directly targeting the family's urgent need for returning to a normal routine and emotional balance makes it the BEST choice for immediate assistance.

**Question Type:** Reasoning

**Content Area:** Human Development, Diversity, and Behavior in the Environment (The effects of life events, stressors, and crises on individuals, families, groups, organizations, and communities)

165. **Correct Answer:** B. Identify support systems and interactions with community resources

**Rationale:** An ecomap is MOST often used to visually depict and analyze a client's social environment, including support systems, relationships, and interactions with community resources. It helps in understanding how various elements of the client's external environment influence well-being and how the client interacts with support systems. While family history and generational patterns can be assessed using tools like a genogram, an ecomap focuses more on the client's current support systems and interactions with external resources rather than historical family dynamics. Evaluating emotional responses and resilience to past traumas is more aligned with clinical assessments and therapeutic interventions rather than the purpose of an ecomap, which is to map out external support and resource connections.

**Question Type:** Application

**Content Area:** Assessment, Diagnosis, and Treatment Planning (Techniques and instruments used to assess clients/client systems)

166. **Correct Answer:** C. Understand any connection between these problems

**Rationale:** In this scenario, the social worker should FIRST focus on understanding the interconnections between the client's chronic health issues, job loss, strained relationships, and spiritual disconnection. This approach allows the social worker to see how these factors interact and influence each other, providing a more comprehensive understanding of the client's overall functioning. By identifying these interconnections, the social worker can develop a more effective intervention plan that addresses the root causes and the interplay of all relevant factors rather than focusing on one issue in isolation. The question asks about the first step in the assessment process so addressing the client's biological health issues is eliminated as this action is an intervention, not an assessment task. Exploring the client's spiritual disconnection is also significant, but it may not be the best initial focus without understanding how it connects to the client's other issues. Spiritual disconnection is often influenced by or influences other aspects of a person's life, such as health, job situation, and relationships. Without first understanding the interplay between all these factors, addressing spiritual disconnection alone might not fully address the root causes or provide a holistic approach to the client's situation.

**Question Type:** Reasoning

**Content Area:** Human Development, Diversity, and Behavior in the Environment (The interplay of biological, psychological, social, and spiritual factors)

167. **Correct Answer:** B. Difficulty in forming peer relationships

**Rationale:** In situations where a child is parentified and takes on responsibilities typically handled by parents, the child is burdened with emotional and practical tasks that are beyond developmental capacity. This role reversal can lead to difficulty in forming healthy peer relationships, as the child may struggle to relate to peers who do not share the same level of responsibility or may lack the time and emotional energy to engage in typical childhood social activities. While resilience in adulthood might seem like a possible outcome for a child who has taken on adult responsibilities at a young age, it is not the most likely consequence of a dysfunctional role reversal. Instead of fostering resilience, this premature burden can create emotional stress and deprive the child of essential childhood experiences, potentially leading to long-term psychological issues. Poor self-image could also result from parentification, especially if the child feels overwhelmed or inadequate in meeting these adult responsibilities. However, the most direct and observable consequence of this role reversal is difficulty in forming peer relationships. This is because the child may become isolated from peers due to their adult-like responsibilities and emotional burdens, which can hinder their ability to connect with others in age-appropriate ways. This difficulty in socialization often has immediate impacts on the child's development, making it the MOST likely consequence in this scenario.

**Question Type:** Application

**Content Area:** Human Development, Diversity, and Behavior in the Environment (Role theories)

168. **Correct Answer:** A. Journaling

**Rationale:** Self-reporting methods involve clients providing personal accounts of experiences, thoughts, and feelings. Journaling is a self-reporting method because it requires the client to document personal reflections and experiences. Behavioral tracking involves monitoring and recording behaviors, often through objective measures rather than the client's subjective reports. Observation involves the social worker directly watching and recording the client's behavior, which is an external assessment method rather than a self-report.

**Question Type:** Recall

**Content Area:** Assessment, Diagnosis, and Treatment Planning (Techniques and instruments used to assess clients/client systems)

169. **Correct Answer:** B. Disinhibited social engagement disorder (DSED)

**Rationale:** DSED is BEST characterized by a pattern of overly familiar behavior with strangers and difficulties in forming secure attachments, which aligns with the symptoms described in the scenario. This disorder often arises in children who have experienced severe neglect or disruptions in early attachment relationships. RAD involves severe emotional withdrawal and difficulties with attachment but does not typically include overly familiar behavior with strangers. PTSD involves reexperiencing traumatic events, avoidance, and heightened arousal but does not specifically include the attachment and social engagement issues described in the scenario.

**Question Type:** Application

**Content Area:** Assessment, Diagnosis, and Treatment Planning (The use of the Diagnostic and Statistical Manual of the American Psychiatric Association)

170. **Correct Answer:** B. The child may act differently during the class session due to the knowledge of being observed.

**Rationale:** The MOST likely concern of the social worker is that the child may modify behavior during the observation, knowing that they are being watched by someone they are familiar with and have worked with before. This situation is related to the Hawthorne effect and the observer effect, both of which describe changes in behavior due to the awareness of being observed. The child's excitement about the classroom visit, combined with the knowledge of being observed by a trusted social worker, may lead to behavior that is not representative of typical performance. This could skew the social worker's assessment and affect the validity of the recommendation for more mainstream activities. While it is important for a social worker to maintain a positive relationship with the child, this is not the primary concern in the context of the observation. The task is to assess the child's readiness for more mainstream activities, and the potential impact on the relationship is secondary to ensuring an accurate assessment. Additionally, the social worker's role often involves making decisions that may not always align with the child's desires but are in the child's best interest. While collaboration with other professionals is essential, the social worker's observation is a critical part of the assessment process and can provide valuable insights. The social worker is trained to conduct such assessments independently, and gathering observations is part of forming an informed opinion. Therefore, the concern about needing to consult other professionals before forming an opinion is not the most pressing issue in this scenario.

**Question Type:** Reasoning

**Content Area:** Assessment, Diagnosis, and Treatment Planning (The principles of active listening and observation)

# Evaluation of Results

| Overall Results of Clinical Test | | | | |
|---|---|---|---|---|
| Content Area | Question Numbers | Number of Questions | Number Correct | Percentage Correct |
| Human Development, Diversity, and Behavior in the Environment (24%) | 2, 15, 16, 22, 24, 34, 35, 38, 40, 41, 42, 50, 53, 55, 58, 60, 63, 66, 73, 80, 83, 85, 90, 91, 94, 106, 111, 114, 116, 119, 121, 146, 150, 151, 153, 155, 160, 161, 164, 166, 167 | 41 | ___/41 | ___% |
| Assessment, Diagnosis, and Treatment Planning (30%) | 1, 3, 6, 7, 9, 10, 11, 12, 13, 14, 20, 21, 37, 43, 52, 59, 64, 67, 74, 75, 77, 79, 84, 88, 95, 96, 100, 112, 115, 120, 124, 125, 127, 128, 130, 131, 140, 145, 147, 148, 149, 152, 154, 156, 157, 159, 162, 165, 168, 169, 170 | 51 | ___/51 | ___% |
| Psychotherapy, Clinical Interventions, and Case Management (27%) | 4, 5, 8, 23, 26, 28, 30, 31, 33, 44, 51, 54, 56, 57, 61, 62, 68, 69, 78, 81, 82, 86, 87, 89, 93, 99, 101, 102, 105, 107, 109, 113, 117, 122, 123, 126, 129, 132, 133, 134, 136, 138, 139, 141, 143, 144 | 46 | ___/46 | ___% |
| Professional Values and Ethics (19%) | 17, 18, 19, 25, 27, 29, 32, 36, 39, 45, 46, 47, 48, 49, 65, 70, 71, 72, 76, 92, 97, 98, 103, 104, 108, 110, 118, 135, 137, 142, 158, 163 | 32 | ___/32 | ___% |
| Overall Clinical Examination Knowledge | ------ | 170 | ___/170 | % |

test: (or umbrella)
- holistic approach first
- ethics: resolve disputes & affected parties
- test: careful, what's the TX phase
- test: translate macro qs to micro practice
- Naltrexone - reduce cravings, Antabus - alc taste bad, methadone - detox opiates
- intake = 1As team
- bio psycho social = interconnectedness
- ego psych: self-identity + self-worth in present moment
Erikson's stages, personality thru social constructs
Hartmann